JEWISH MARRIAGES AND THE ENGLISH LAW

BY

H. S. Q. HENRIQUES, M.A., B.C.L.

OF THE NORTHERN CIRCUIT, BARRISTER-AT-LAW
FORMERLY SCHOLAR OF WORCESTER COLLEGE
AND VINERIAN SCHOLAR IN THE UNIVERSITY OF OXFORD

Reprinted from the JEWISH QUARTERLY REVIEW *of April, 1908*
with additions and corrections

THE LAWBOOK EXCHANGE, LTD.
Clark, New Jersey
2006

ISBN-13: 978-1-58477-642-0
ISBN-10: 1-58477-642-0

Printed in the United States of America on acid-free paper

THE LAWBOOK EXCHANGE, LTD.
33 Terminal Avenue
Clark, New Jersey 07066-1321

Please see our website for a selection of our other publications and fine facsimile reprints of classic works of legal history:
www.lawbookexchange.com

Library of Congress Cataloging-in-Publication Data

Henriques, H. S. Q. (Henry Straus Quixano), 1866-1925.
Jewish marriages and the English law / Henriques, H.S.Q.
p. cm.
Originally published: London : Bibliophile Press, 1909.
Includes bibliographical references and index.
ISBN 1-58477-642-0 (alk. paper)
1. Marriage law--England. 2. Jews--Legal status, laws, etc.--England. 3. Marriage (Jewish law) I. Title.
KD755.H46 2005
346.4201'6--dc22

2005026307

JEWISH MARRIAGES AND THE ENGLISH LAW

BY

H. S. Q. HENRIQUES, M.A., B.C.L.

OF THE NORTHERN CIRCUIT, BARRISTER-AT-LAW
FORMERLY SCHOLAR OF WORCESTER COLLEGE
AND VINERIAN SCHOLAR IN THE UNIVERSITY OF OXFORD

Reprinted from the JEWISH QUARTERLY REVIEW *of April, 1908*
with additions and corrections

THE BIBLIOPHILE PRESS
149 EDGWARE ROAD, LONDON, W.
1909

OXFORD: HORACE HART
PRINTER TO THE UNIVERSITY

JEWISH MARRIAGES AND THE ENGLISH LAW.

At the present time the validity of Jewish marriages celebrated in England is expressly declared by several Acts of Parliament; the question how far such marriages are valid, apart from this statutory sanction, is one of considerable difficulty. Moreover, the proper interpretation of the Marriage Acts, so far as they concern Jewish marriages, is an interesting but by no means easy subject.

Recognition by English law in the pre-expulsion period of marriages solemnized in accordance with the *lex Judaica*.

There is evidence that Jewish marriages were recognized for some purposes by the law of the land in the days before the expulsion of the Jews by Edward I, for there are at least two cases cited in books of acknowledged authority in early law. The first is as follows. A Jew born in England purchased land and married a Jewess. The husband was converted to the Christian faith and died. His widow, who had not been converted, claimed her dower. It was resolved in Parliament that she should not have dower because she had refused to be converted with her husband [1].

[1] Co. Lit., 31 b, 32 a. Jenkins, 8 *Cent. of Reports*, p. 3, case 2 (in the margin). Tovey, *Anglia Judaica*, p. 230. The latter gives the entry of the close rolls at length. It is as follows:

"Ostensum est regi, ex parte Isaac de Cantuar. Judaei, quod cum emerit de Abbate Sancti Augustini Cantuar. quandam domum in Cantuaria, quae fuit Augustini Conversi, et quam idem Augustinus postquam se converterat, dederat praedictae domui Sancti Augustini, Chera Judaea, quae fuit uxor praedicti Augustini, petit versus praedictum Isaac dotem suam de domo praedicta. Quia vero contra justitiam est, quod ipsa Chera dotem petat vel habeat de tenemento quod fuit ipsius viri sui, *ex quo in conversione sua noluit ei adhaerere et cum eo converti* Mandatum est Justiciar. ad custodiam Judaeorum assignat. &c., quod si ita est, de caetero placitum inde non teneant.

T. R. apud Cant. 5 die Aprilis, Claus. 18 H. 3, m. 17 dorso."

This case was decided in the year 1234, nearly sixty years before the expulsion; the other case occurred nine years after that event, and is also concerned with the marriages of Jews who had subsequently been converted to Christianity. In the year 1299, an Essex jury found that Henry de Winton and his wife had married according to Jewish law, and afterwards become Christians and had issue, a son Thomas, who, they find, is the heir, provided that the marriage solemnized before the conversion can be held good[1].

The question, no doubt, in both these cases was the effect upon a Jewish marriage of the conversion to Christianity of one or both the parties to it, and it was definitely decided that where one of the spouses only became a convert he could treat the marriage as null and void, on the ground that a true believer was not bound to live in wedlock with an infidel, so that the spouse who remained unconverted lost all the rights which the marriage would have otherwise conferred[2]. Where both spouses were converted, the question whether the marriage remained valid or not seems to have been unsettled at the time of the expulsion. It was probably not frequently raised, for it could only be of importance where property was claimed,

[1] *Calend. Geneal.*, II, 563. *Inq. Post. Mort.*, 27 Edw. I, no. 12. The record is as follows:

"Juratores dicunt quod dictus Henricus de Winton duxit quandam in uxorem sub lege Judaica, et postea conversi erant ad legem Christianam. Et generabant quendam filium, Thomam nomine, quem dicunt esse haeredem propinquiorem ipsius Henrici si matrimonium praecontractum inter ipsos antequam conversi essent rite stare posset. Item dicunt quod dictus Thomas est aetatis triginta annorum et amplius. Essex."

[2] A Jewish widow's right to dower, and therefore, by implication, the validity of her marriage was undoubtedly recognized, see the addenda to Jacob's edition of Roper on Husband and Wife, p. 476 (note). Prynne gives a writ to the justices of the Jews in 23 Hen. III, directing them to put the two sons of one Samuel, a deceased Jew, into possession of his lands and chattels on payment of a fine, "salvo uxori ejusdem Samuelis rationabili dote sua, secundum legem et consuetudinem Judaeorum," p. 27.

and the rule of feudal law, which was strictly enforced, was that by the ceremony of conversion the whole of the convert's property passed to the Crown. It was for this reason that the *Domus Conversorum* or Hospice for the maintenance of Jewish converts was established by Henry III in 1232[1]. Henry of Winton had apparently acquired land after his conversion, but most of the Jewish converts spent the remainder of their days in the *Domus Conversorum* as pensioners upon the royal bounty.

Decision of the House of Lords in 1844 that the presence of a clergyman in holy orders was by the common law necessary to the validity of a marriage.

These cases are cited here to show that in these ancient times a marriage of Jews, according to the *lex Judaica*, was recognized even in the case of claims to land by a widow in respect of her dower or a son in respect of his inheritance. This recognition is the more important, because in the case of such claims the lay courts of law required strict proof of an alleged marriage, and refused to recognize the marriage of Christians unless it was celebrated *in facie ecclesiae*, or at least in the presence of an ordained clergyman. Indeed, as a result of the decision in the Queen *v.* Millis[2], the English lawyer is bound to assume that in all cases where the existence of a marriage was in issue, the ordinary courts of law were more strict than the ecclesiastical courts, which, in accordance with the canon law that prevailed throughout Christendom, considered that any contract *per verba de praesenti* (i.e. where the parties acknowledged each other as man and wife), and even a contract *per verba de futuro*, if followed by cohabitation, constituted a valid marriage, although neither made in church nor in the presence of a priest. No doubt the parties to such clandestine and irregular marriages were held to have committed an ecclesiastical offence and were liable to the censures of the Church, and to be compelled by the spiritual court, at least after the time of Pope Innocent III and the Lateran Council (A.D. 1215), to

[1] See J. M. Rigg, *Select Pleas, Starrs, &c.*, from the Exchequer of the Jews, p. xxxvi.

[2] (1844), 10 C. & F., 534.

solemnize their marriage *in facie ecclesiae*[1], but the marriage itself was for many purposes held valid. It was not until the Council of Trent, the decrees of which were not made binding in England, issued the "Decretum de reformatione matrimonii" in the year 1563 that the presence of a priest was made essential to the validity of the marriage ceremony[2]. Nevertheless, in the year 1844, after considering all the authorities and consulting the judges, the House of Lords, sitting as the ultimate Court of Appeal, held in the case of the Queen *v.* Millis that by the common law of England from the earliest times the presence of a clergyman in holy orders was absolutely necessary to constitute a valid marriage. It is true that on the question being put the law lords were equally divided, and that the decision not to reverse the decree of the Court below (the Queen's Bench of Ireland) was only arrived at by reason of the ancient rule of the House "semper praesumitur pro negante." Yet the decision is none the less as binding on all the courts of law, including the House of Lords itself, as if it had been arrived at unanimously, and was in fact followed by that House fifteen years later in the case of Beamish *v.* Beamish[3]. Still the diversity of opinion in the highest court shows that the broad principle laid down was by no means at the time universally

[1] See Bunting's case (1585). Moore, 170, also 4 Co. Rep. 29.

[2] Lord Stowell in delivering judgment in Dalrymple *v.* Dalrymple says, "The law of the Church, the canon law, although in conformity with the prevailing theological opinion, it reverenced marriage as a sacrament, still so far respected its natural and civil origin as to consider that where the natural and civil contract was performed it had the full essence of matrimony without the intervention of a priest; it had even in that state the character of a sacrament; for it is a misapprehension to suppose that this intervention was required as matter of necessity, even for that purpose, before the Council of Trent." (2 Hag., *Cons.* 64.) It was, however, a general, if not universal view among churchmen, long before the Council of Trent, that to make a contract of marriage complete for all purposes the sacerdotal benediction was necessary, and Selden ascribes this doctrine to the imitation of pagan and Jewish customs (Ux. Eb., lib. II, cap. 28).

[3] (1861), 9 H. & C., 274.

recognized, and enables the student to doubt its historical accuracy, though the lawyer must admit its binding authority. There are, moreover, dicta of the law lords in the case of Beamish *v.* Beamish which indicate that this principle is not applicable to a case where the presence of a minister in holy orders is impossible, and by parity of reason it may be argued that it extended only to marriages *lege Christiana* and had no application to marriages *lege Judaica*. However, whatever the ancient common law may have been, it may be safely affirmed that in the reign of Charles II the marriage of Christians was not held to be valid unless it was celebrated in the presence of a duly ordained clergyman. During the Great Rebellion and the Commonwealth, the system of solemnizing marriages in the presence of a justice of the peace had been established, and, indeed, in those times it would have been difficult, if not impossible, to secure the presence of a duly ordained minister at every marriage; upon the Restoration, therefore, it was thought necessary for the Convention Parliament, which was afterwards confirmed by the following Parliament, to pass a public Act for the confirmation of these marriages, which, in the terms of the statute, were to be adjudged, esteemed, and taken to be of the same effect as if they had been solemnized according to the rites and ceremonies established or used in the Church or kingdom of England any law, custom, or usage to the contrary notwithstanding[1].

The existence of this statute undoubtedly indicates the

[1] 12 Car. II, c. 33, and 13 Car. II, st. 1, c. 11. The ordinance of the Commonwealth is cap. 6 of 1653 called "An Act touching Marriages and the Registering thereof and also touching Births and Burials," passed by Barebone's Parliament on August 24, 1656, and confirmed by the second Protectorate Parliament in 1656 by the Act cap. 10 of that year. See Scobell, vol. II, p. 236 and p. 394. Previously by the Directory for Public Worship, which was substituted for the Book of Common Prayer by an ordinance of the Long Parliament passed in March 164$\frac{4}{5}$, marriages were to be solemnized "by a lawful Minister of the Word" and registered by him. See Scobell, I, p. 86.

prevalence of the theory, at the time when it was enacted, that the presence of a clergyman in holy orders was necessary for the legal validity of a marriage, and there are cases in the reports which show that this was not merely a popular theory, but one which was fully recognized and acted upon in the Courts. For example, in the case of Haydon *v.* Gould, which was decided by the Court of Delegates in the year 1711, it was held that a husband married in a Sabbatarian congregation, by one of its ministers, was not entitled to letters of administration to the estate of his dead wife, because the minister who solemnized the marriage was a mere layman and not in orders, and therefore the marriage was void[1]. On the other hand, the clergyman whose presence was required need not be a minister of the Church of England, for it would suffice if a person in holy orders, recognized by that church, such as a Roman Catholic or Greek priest, were present[2]. But apart from the presence of a priest, or after the Reformation a deacon duly ordained, no religious ceremony or other formality was required to constitute a valid marriage. All that was necessary was for the parties to the marriage to declare "per verba de praesenti" that they took each other for man and wife. It was universally felt to be desirable that all marriages should take place in open church after due publication of banns or the granting of a licence, and the canon law imposed penalties, enforceable in the ecclesiastical courts, both on the parties to clandestine marriages and the clergyman who solemnized them. But though these secret marriages were branded as irregular, it was not till late that the law declaring them invalid was passed. The earliest legislation imposing the necessity of the publication of banns was

The other formalities required by the common law for a valid marriage. The publication of banns not indispensable.

[1] Haydon *v.* Gould (1711), 1 Salk., 119. There are several cases in the books which seem to point in the other direction (notably Jesson *v.* Collins (1704) and Wigmore's Case (1707), 2 Salk., 437), with which may be compared the arguments and some dicta in the judgment in this case.

[2] See Beau Fielding's Case (1706), 14 St. Tr. 1327, and Rex *v.* the Inhabitants of Brampton (1808), 10 East, 282 at p. 288.

enacted for the purpose of assisting the revenue. In 1695, certain duties to be paid upon marriages were granted to the Crown for the purpose of meeting the expenses of the French War, and in order to prevent the evasion of this tax, which the publicity of the marriage ceremony would render more difficult, it was enacted that every clergyman solemnizing a marriage without banns or licence should be liable to forfeit one hundred pounds [1]. As means of evading the provisions of this enactment seem to have been discovered, a further statute was passed in the following year confirming the forfeiture imposed upon clergymen celebrating such marriages, and also rendering the parties to such marriages liable to a penalty of ten pounds, and the clerk or sexton assisting at their celebration to a forfeiture of five pounds [2]. The tax upon marriages was only imposed for a period of five years, but the penal sections of these statutes were not repealed. Nevertheless, they do not seem to have been enforced, for clandestine marriages continued to be so frequent that great loss occurred to the revenue by the non-payment of the duty of five shillings imposed upon every piece of paper or parchment upon which a licence or certificate of marriage was engrossed.

Accordingly in the year 1711 the legislature again intervened, and again imposed a forfeiture of one hundred pounds upon every parson, vicar, curate, or other person in holy orders, beneficed or not beneficed, who performed a marriage without banns or licence [3]. These measures did not declare secret marriages void, and in consequence failed to put an end to the evil. For though such marriages no longer took place in churches, there was a class of penniless and degraded clergymen who boldly defied the penalties of

[1] 6 & 7 Will. III, c. 6, s. 52.

[2] 7 & 8 Will. III, c. 35.

[3] 10 Ann, c. 18 (c. 19, Ruff.), ss. 176-8. The necessity for passing this enactment seems to have been that the earlier statutes punished only clergymen with benefices.

the statute, and it was well known that the "Fleet" and "Hedge" parsons drove a roaring trade. To do away with this scandal, and otherwise amend the matrimonial law, Lord Hardwicke's Marriage Act of 1753 (26 Geo. II, c. 23) was passed. It is entitled "an Act for the better preventing of clandestine marriages," and provides that all marriages solemnized in any other place than a church or public chapel, in which banns have been published, or for which a marriage licence has been obtained, unless by special licence granted by the Archbishop of Canterbury[1], shall be null and void to all intents and purposes whatsoever. The Act also abolished the jurisdiction of the ecclesiastical courts specifically to enforce a contract to marry, and laid down regulations for the publication of banns and issue of licences, and the registration of marriages, and made it felony for any person to solemnize matrimony in contravention of the provisions of the Act or to make a false entry in, or destroy a marriage register, or to forge a marriage licence. But it is expressly declared that the Act shall not extend to the marriages of any of the royal family, or to marriages in Scotland, or beyond the seas, or to the marriages amongst the people called Quakers or persons professing the Jewish religion.

Lord Hardwicke's Marriage Act, 1753.

Lord Hardwicke's Act effectually put an end to many of the evils against which it was aimed, for in future all marriages celebrated in England, excepting those of Jews and Quakers, had to take place in a recognized church in the presence of two or more witnesses in addition to the officiating clergyman, and, moreover, sufficient means of inquiry as to the validity of any contemplated marriage were secured by the publication of banns or the procedure necessary for obtaining a marriage licence. But the Act produced other hardships and inconveniences which, after a lapse of seventy years, it was found necessary to remedy. Decrees of nullity of marriage were too easily obtainable,

Lord Hardwicke's Act repealed by the Marriage Act of 1823.

[1] Which power is given by 25 Hen. VIII, c. 21 (the Peter Pence and Dispensations Act, 1533).

for the marriages of minors, celebrated without the consent of their parents or guardians, were declared null and void. Furthermore, a marriage was absolutely invalidated by a flaw or error in the publication of the banns or other necessary preliminary to it, even as against wholly innocent parties or where the error or omission had been caused wilfully or fraudulently by one of the spouses without the knowledge or connivance of the other. Accordingly the Marriage Act, 1823 (4 Geo. IV, c. 76)[1], was passed. It repealed, and to a great extent re-enacted, Lord Hardwicke's Act, and with some amendments is in force at the present time, and regulates almost all marriages celebrated in the churches or chapels belonging to the established Church. The main alterations in the law which it effected are as follows. The marriage of minors without the consent of their parents or guardians was not to be null and void, but the guilty party by whom the marriage without the requisite consent was procured, was made liable to forfeit any property coming to him or her by virtue of the marriage. Indeed, as marriage was declared to be invalid only where both the parties to it "knowingly and wilfully" intermarried in a place where banns may not be lawfully published, or without due publication of banns or a licence, or "knowingly and wilfully" consented or acquiesced in the solemnization of their marriage by a person not being in holy orders. Other regulations were that no marriage should take place more than three months after the publication of banns or granting of the licence, that the marriage is to be solemnized in a church in which the banns have been published or which is named in the licence, and there are also provisions as to the residence of the parties to the marriage in the parish in which it is celebrated, and as to the due publication of banns or application for a licence. Like Lord Hardwicke's Act, the operation

[1] For the circumstances attending the passage of this Act see Walpole's *History of England from* 1815, vol. II, pp. 75-9.

of the Marriage Act of 1823 was confined to England, and did not extend to the marriages of Quakers or Jews.

In five exceptional cases marriages not in the parish church still recognized as valid.

Thus after the year 1753 there was practically only one form of marriage known to the law, namely a marriage in the parish church in accordance with the forms and rubrics of the Church of England, and after due compliance with the provisions of the Marriage Acts as to the publication of banns or the issue of licences. There were only five exceptions, namely, (1) where a special licence had been obtained from the Archbishop of Canterbury, but, apart from the question of expense, such licences would only be given in exceptional cases; (2) the marriages of members of the royal family; (3) marriages solemnized beyond the borders of England; in such cases, if the marriage takes place in a foreign country with a settled system of law that recognizes Christian marriage, it is sufficient if the formalities required by the law of that country are complied with, provided that the parties, if domiciled in England, are not prohibited by our law from intermarrying. Thus the law of Scotland recognizes irregular marriages, and does not require the presence of a clergyman to make a marriage valid, and therefore after the passage of the Marriage Acts clandestine marriages could still take place among persons domiciled in England, if they adopted the simple expedient of crossing the Scotch border, and the village of Gretna Green became notorious for its runaway marriages celebrated in the presence of the blacksmith. This scandal was finally put an end to by Lord Brougham's Act of 1856 (19 & 20 Vict., c. 96), which provides that an irregular marriage contracted in Scotland shall not be valid unless one of the parties to it has his ordinary place of residence in Scotland or has lived there for twenty-one days immediately preceding the marriage[1]. On the other

[1] For the Scotch irregular marriage see Dalrymple *v.* Dalrymple (1811), 2 Hag., *Con.* 54. For the validity of the Gretna Green marriages see Gardner *v.* the Attorney General (1889), 60 L.T., p. 839.

band, these marriages solemnized abroad must be accompanied with all the formalities required by the *lex loci actus*, or otherwise they will be held invalid here, unless they are rendered valid by the provisions of some statutory enactment, such as the Foreign Marriage Act of 1892, or by the proper application of the doctrine of exterritoriality [1]. And where a marriage takes place outside British territory, but in a place where there is no local law which governs Christian marriages, or where it is practically impossible for British subjects to comply with the local law, compliance with the very scanty requirements of the ancient common law of England will then be sufficient to constitute a valid marriage, and it would seem that the presence of an ordained clergyman may be dispensed with, if none can be found within a reasonable distance of the place in which the marriage is performed [2].

(4) Marriages amongst the people called Quakers. This privilege was at first confined to cases where both parties to the marriage were members of the Society of Friends, but is now extended to cases where one of the spouses only, or where neither of them is a member of the Society, provided that a certificate, signed by a registering officer of the Society of Friends, stating that the party on whose behalf notice of marriage is given is authorized thereto by the rules of the Society, is produced to the superintendent

[1] See Kent *v.* Burgess (1840), 11 Sim., p. 361, where a marriage between British subjects, performed by a clergyman of the Church of England at the English Church at Antwerp, in the presence of the British Consul, was held invalid on the ground that certain ceremonies prescribed by the law of Belgium had not been observed. The Foreign Marriage Act, 1892 (55 & 56 Vict., c. 23), repeals and consolidates a number of earlier Acts from 1823 onwards, known as the Foreign Marriage and Consular Marriage Acts. For its effect see Hay *v.* Northcote, L. R. [1900], 2 Ch., 262.

[2] See the Confirmation of Marriages on Her Majesty's Ships Act, 1879 (42 & 43 Vict., c. 29), and Culling *v.* Culling, L. R. [1896] P. 116, and Ruding *v.* Smith (1821), 2 Hag., *Con.* 371, and Westlake's *Private International Law*, §§ 26–32.

registrar to whom notice of intention to solemnize such marriage is given [1].

(5) Marriages amongst persons professing the Jewish religion, where both parties to the marriage profess that religion. These marriages will be dealt with in detail later.

The Dissenter's Marriage Act, 1836.

Thus, with the few exceptions here enumerated, all persons, whatever their religious creed, were compelled to celebrate their marriages in one of the churches or chapels belonging to the Church of England, and in accordance with the rites and ceremonies of that Church. This in the course of time came to be recognized as a great hardship, both to Roman Catholics and Protestant Nonconformists, and in the year 1836 an Act of Parliament to remove this grievance was introduced and carried by Lord John Russell. By this statute a wholly new form of marriage was established, namely, marriage by a Registrar's certificate, and the purely civil character of matrimony was fully recognized, for the former requirements of the presence of a clergyman in holy orders, an ecclesiastical licence, or the publication of banns, and attendance at church, once essential to a valid marriage, were no longer insisted upon. The Marriage Act of 1836 (6 & 7 Will. IV, c. 85) enabled all persons to intermarry by giving due notice to, and obtaining a certificate from, the superintendent registrar for the district in which one of the parties to the intended marriage resides. The superintendent registrar files the notice of marriage when given to him, and enters a copy of it in the Marriage Notice Book, which is open to public inspection. In order to give full publicity to these marriages, it was originally provided that all these notices of marriage should be read at the next weekly meeting of the Guardians of the Poor Law Union, but this provision proving irksome, it was repealed by the Marriage and Registration Act of 1856 (19 & 20 Vict., c. 119), which enacted instead that

[1] See The Marriage (Society of Friends) Acts, 1860 and 1872 (23 & 24 Vict., c. 18, and 35 Vict., c. 10).

the notice of marriage, unless it was to be by licence, should be suspended in the office of the superintendent registrar for a period of twenty-one days. There are also clauses enabling persons, whose consent is required by law, to prevent a marriage by writing "forbidden" opposite the notice in the marriage notice book, or any member of the public to enter a caveat against a marriage (ss. 9 and 13). The superintendent registrar may issue his certificate after the expiration of twenty-one days from the entry of the notice, or if it is accompanied with a licence, after seven days, which latter period has by the Marriage and Registration Act of 1856 been reduced to one whole day. The certificate which is in force only for three months from the entry of the marriage notice, authorizes the solemnization of the marriage at the place named in it. The place may be either a church or a place of religious worship registered for the solemnization of marriages, or if the parties do not desire a religious ceremony, the office of the superintendent registrar, and except in the case of marriages in a church, where the marriage must be celebrated according to the rites of the Church of England, or where the parties are Jews or Quakers, for whom special provision is made, every such marriage shall be solemnized with open doors between the hours of eight and twelve in the forenoon (now extended to three in the afternoon by the Marriage Act of 1886, 49 & 50 Vict., c. 14, s. 1), in the presence of some registrar of the district and two or more credible witnesses. The registrar in whose presence the marriage is solemnized must forthwith register the marriage in the book supplied by the Registrar-General for that purpose, and the entry must be signed by the person (if any) solemnizing the marriage, the registrar himself, and both the parties to the marriage, and attested by two witnesses. Certified copies of this marriage register book are to be sent periodically to the Registrar-General. Persons unduly solemnizing marriages are declared guilty of felony, but from this provision the marriages of Jews and Quakers are expressly excepted; and marriages unduly solemnized with the knowledge of both parties are declared null and void.

The Births and Deaths Registration Act, 1836.

The Act is to be read in connexion with the one immediately following it in the statute book, namely the Births and Deaths Registration Act, 1836 (6 & 7 Will. IV, c. 86), which provides for the appointment of registrars and the due registration of marriages. The following year it was found necessary to pass an Act to explain and amend these two statutes [1], and a few years later the Marriage Act of 1840 (3 & 4 Vict., c. 72) was passed to provide for the solemnization of marriages in the districts in or near which the parties reside, but the provisions of this Act are not to apply to the marriages of Quakers or persons professing the Jewish religion. Still further amendments were introduced by the Marriage and Registration Act of 1856 (19 & 20 Vict., c. 119), which abolished the requirement that all notices of marriage should be read before the Poor Law Guardians, and enacts that every notice of marriage should be accompanied by a declaration subscribed by the party giving it, that he or she believes that there is no impediment or lawful hindrance to the marriage, and lays down further regulations as to marriage notices and licences, the mode of solemnizing marriages in registered buildings, the subsequent addition of a religious ceremony where a marriage has been contracted at a registry office, the granting of licences for marriages in districts in which neither of the parties resides, and ordains the penalties of perjury against those who knowingly and wilfully make any false declaration or sign any false notice for the purpose of procuring a marriage, and further renders any person who thus fraudulently procures a marriage liable to forfeit any estate or interest in any property that might thereby accrue to him. There are further provisions enabling Quakers and Jews to solemnize their marriages by licence, and also special regulations as to the West

The Marriage and Registration Act, 1856.

[1] See the Births and Deaths Registration Act, 1837 (7 Will. IV & 1 Vict., c. 22).

London Synagogue of British Jews, which will be dealt with more particularly hereafter. The Marriage Act of 1886 (49 & 50 Vict., c. 14) extended the time for solemnizing marriages from noon to three in the afternoon, and the Marriage Act of 1898 (61 & 62 Vict., c. 58) still further increased the facilities for the marriage of Dissenters by dispensing with the attendance of the registrar, which was required by the Marriage Act of 1836, provided that the marriage is solemnized in a building registered under the Act of 1836 for solemnizing marriages, and in the presence of an "authorized person," i.e. a person who has been certified to the Registrar-General as having been duly authorized for the purpose by the trustees or other governing body of the registered building. The Act lays the duty of registering the marriage in due course upon such authorized person. Marriages in accordance with the practice and usages of the Society of Friends, or of persons professing the Jewish religion, are expressly excluded from the operation of this Act also, and the Act is in all cases optional, for the attendance of the district registrar at any registered building may still be required by persons desiring to be married, although an authorized person has been appointed under the provisions of the Act.

The Marriage Act, 1898.

As our law stands, Jews may avail themselves of any of these forms of marriage[1], but in most cases Jewish marriages are contracted under the special provisions made for Jews by the Marriage Act of 1836, and the Marriage and Registration Act of 1856. Before, however, discussing these, it will not be out of place to consider the position of Jewish marriages at the period preceding these enactments. Reasons have already been given for holding that prior to the expulsion of the Jews from England, their marriages, though solemnized in accordance with the *lex Judaica*, and without the presence of a priest as required by the *lex Christiana*, were considered legally binding for many purposes. After

The validity of Jewish marriages before the Marriage Acts.

[1] See Jones *v.* Robinson (1815), 2 Phil., p. 285.

the return of the Jews to England in the reign of Charles II, it is an undoubted fact that they continued to contract marriages in accordance with their own usages, and although there is little authority upon the subject, so far as cases actually decided in the courts of law are concerned, the opinion current amongst legal writers and the profession seems to have been that these marriages were valid. Mr. Jacob, in the Addenda to the second edition of Roper's *Husband and Wife*, which was published in the year 1826, writes upon this subject, "With respect to the Jews, it appears that their marriages have at all times been celebrated according to the rites of their own religion, and the legal validity of such marriages has been recognized in various cases, as well before as since the Marriage Act. And questions arising upon them are determined by the Jewish law, which is ascertained in the same manner as a foreign law, by the testimony of its professors. This exception to the general law has probably arisen from the peculiarities attending the state of the Jewish nation in England: having always been looked upon as a distinct people, and having for a long time been treated rather as aliens, than as native subjects. During the earlier periods of their residence in England, they were so far severed from the rest of the inhabitants as to be subjected to a distinct judicature" (the Exchequer of the Jews), "regulated to a certain extent by their own laws [1]."

Doubts thrown on the validity of Jewish marriages.

6 & 7 Will. III, c. 6.

Although this was the opinion of those learned in the law, there was undoubtedly a very widespread popular feeling that these marriages, not being celebrated in the presence of an ordained clergyman, were null and void. On one important occasion this view became embodied in an Act of Parliament. The statute 6 & 7 Will. III, c. 6, entitled "an Act for granting to His Majesty certain rates and duties upon marriages, births and burials, and upon batchelors and widowers for the term of five years for

[1] Roper's *Husband and Wife*, 2nd edition, vol. II, pp. 475–6.

carrying on the war against France with vigour," among other things imposed a tax of two shillings and sixpence on the marriage of every person not in receipt of alms, and additional taxes upon the marriage of persons of rank or property, ranging from fifty pounds in the case of a duke to ten shillings in the case of the son of a man having real estate to the value of fifty pounds per annum or personal estate of six hundred pounds or upwards. In order to prevent the payment of this tax being evaded by Jews and others on the ground that the liability to pay it did not attach to a union which was not recognized by law as a valid marriage, two clauses were added at the end of the statute in the following terms: "Provided always and be it further enacted by the authority aforesaid That all persons commonly called Quakers or reputed such and all Papists or reputed Papists whether they are Popish recusants convict or not and all Jews or any other persons who shall cohabit and live together as man and wife shall and are hereby made lyable to pay the several and respective duties and sums of money payable upon marriages according to their respective degrees titles orders and qualifications as they ought to have paid by virtue of this Act if they had been married according to the Law of England which duties and sums of money shall be collected levied and paid in such manner and subject to such rules and directions and under such penalties and forfeitures as are in this Act specified and contained . . . And upon every pretended marriage which shall be made by any such person within the said term of five years according to the method and forms used amongst them the man so entering into such pretended state of matrimony shall within five days after give notice thereof to the collectors or one of them of the parish or place where he lives and in default of giving such notice he shall forfeit the sum of five pounds one moiety thereof to the King's Majesty the other moiety to the informer."

The legislature was, moreover, careful to declare that

the liability of such unions to taxation should not be taken to confer upon them any legal sanction or validity, and accordingly the final clause of the statute is worded as follows: "Provided always that nothing herein contained shall be construed to make good or effectual in law any such marriage or pretended marriage but that they shall be of the same force and virtue and no other as they would have been if this Act had never been made."

The legal position of Roman Catholic, Quaker, and Jewish marriages compared.

It is to be observed that this Act of Parliament deals with the marriages of Quakers, Papists and Jews as if they were in precisely the same legal position. But there is little doubt that until the enactment of Lord Hardwicke's Marriage Act in the year 1753 the marriage of Papists by their own priests would be recognized as valid in law. Of such marriages Sir Edward Simpson, in delivering the judgment of the Court in the well-known case of Scrimshire *v.* Scrimshire in the year 1752, says: "By the law of this country it is, I apprehend, prohibited under severe penalties for a Roman Catholic priest to be in this country and to exercise any part of his office as a Popish priest in this kingdom. But as a priest popishly ordained is allowed to be a legal presbyter, it is generally said that a marriage by a Popish priest is good; and it is true, when it is celebrated after the English ritual, for he is allowed to be a priest[1]." On the other hand, the weight of legal authority seems to incline to the invalidity of Quakers' marriages prior to the year 1753, and since the decision of the Queen *v.* Millis (1844), 10 Cl. & F., 534, it can hardly be successfully contended that such marriages were legal, for Quakers, though Christians, do not recognize any distinct priests or ministers. It is said that Sir Mathew Hale, when Chief Baron, had pronounced in favour of a Quaker's marriage, and he is bitterly attacked by Roger North in his *Life of Lord Keeper Guilford* for

[1] Hag., *Cons.*, vol. II, p. 400; see also Beau Fielding's case (1706), 14 St. Tr., 1327; R. *v.* the Inhabitants of Brampton (1808), 10 East, p. 282; and Lautour *v.* Teesdale (1816), 8 Taunt., 830.

having done so; but this does not appear to be a fair representation of that learned judge's decision, and some years later in the case of Green *v.* Green, which was a suit for the restitution of conjugal rights instituted by a Quaker, the libel was dismissed because the parties had not been married according to the forms of the Church of England[1]. In the third place, Jewish marriages were valid because of the recognition which had anciently been accorded to the *lex Judaica* in matrimonial questions. We have already observed from the perusal of the case in Lilly's *Practical Register*, which is discussed in "The Jews and the English Law[2]," that the law concerning the Jews as administered before their expulsion was applied to them after their return, so far as the altered circumstances of the times would permit. The Courts would have had no reason for disregarding the ancient decisions from which the recognition of the validity of Jewish marriages in feudal times must be inferred. Indeed, where questions concerning Jewish marriages, solemnized before the passing of Lord Hardwicke's Act, came before the Courts, it seems to have been taken for granted that such marriages were binding although not celebrated in the presence of any one in holy orders. To illustrate this, let us take the three cases which are mentioned in the books. The case of Franks *v.* Martin came before the House of Lords in the year 1760, and was a dispute as to the effect of a covenant contained in a settlement made on the marriage of Isaac Franks with the daughter of Moses Hart, solemnized in the year 1720 by Aaron Hart, the chief rabbi of the German Jews and uncle of the bride. The covenant was interpreted and enforced by the Court, but if the marriage had been invalid, the covenant would have been unenforceable,

Cases touching the validity of Jewish marriages before 1753.

[1] See North's *Life of Guilford*, p. 68; Burnet's *Life of Hale*, p. 44; Campbell's *Lives of the Chief Justices of England*, vol. I, pp. 557-8; Roper's *Husband and Wife* (2nd ed.), vol. II, pp. 463-7, and id., pp. 476-80; and Hag., *Cons.*, vol. I, App. p. 9, note.

[2] Pp. 188-9.

and there would have been no occasion to take the case up to the highest court of appeal [1]. The second case is that of Da Costa *v.* Villa Real (1733), which was a suit in the Court of Arches to enforce a contract of marriage between two opulent persons both professing the Jewish religion. The argument that the suit was not maintainable because the parties to it were Jews seems to have been raised, but overruled, and the cause was ultimately dismissed upon the ground that a lady's promise to marry "at the end of the year from her husband's death, if her father should consent" was conditional and not absolute. It is an interesting speculation whether, if the Court had held the promise to be enforceable, it would have decreed that the marriage should be celebrated in a church or in a synagogue [2]. The third and last case is that of Andreas *v.* Andreas, which was tried in 1737. Andreas and his wife were both Jews and were married according to the forms of the Jewish religion: she cited him in a cause for the restitution of conjugal rights. On the admission of the libel, Dr. Strahan objected that, as they had been married according to the forms of the Jewish nation and not of the Church of England, the Court could take no notice of such marriage, and she could not institute such a cause against her husband in the Ecclesiastical Court, and the case of Green *v.* Green (mentioned above), where a Quaker instituted such a suit and the libel was dismissed, was cited. The Court was of opinion, however, that as the parties had contracted such a marriage as would bind them according to the Jewish forms, the woman was

[1] See Franks *v.* Martin (1760), 5 Brown's *Parl. Cas.*, 151. The marriage article in question was contained in a Hebrew document, which it was unsuccessfully contended was an ordinary Ketuba, and therefore binding only on the husband, but not on the bride's father.

[2] See note in Hag., *Cons.*, I, p. 242; an action for damages for breach of promise was afterwards brought at common law, but the plaintiff was non-suited on account of being estopped by the previous judgment of the Court of Arches. See 2 Str., p. 961, and the Duchess of Kingston's case (1776), 20 St. Tr., at p. 397.

entitled to a remedy, and that the proceeding would lie and admitted the libel [1]. On the strength of these authorities, it may fairly be argued that marriages in accordance with the usages of the Jews were valid and legally binding before the year 1753.

Jewish marriages after 1753.

The Act of that year for the better preventing of clandestine marriages, better known as Lord Hardwicke's Marriage Act, contains a special clause dealing with these marriages. It is as follows: "Provided likewise that nothing in this Act contained shall extend to that part of Great Britain called Scotland, nor to any marriages amongst the people called Quakers, or amongst the persons professing the Jewish religion, where both the parties to any such marriage shall be of the people called Quakers or persons professing the Jewish religion respectively, nor to any marriages solemnized beyond the seas [2]."

This clause, though it merely excepts these marriages from the operation of the Marriage Act, was held to be an acknowledgment by the legislature of the validity both of Quaker and Jewish marriages. Thus in the case of Vigevena and Silveira *v.* Alvarez, tried by the Prerogative Court in the year 1794, in which the legitimacy of the offspring of a Jewish marriage was in issue, an objection was raised that persons coming before any ecclesiastical court to claim any right by marriage must show the marriage to have been agreeably to the rites and ceremonies of the Christian Church. The advocates on the other side submitted that this was the first time that the principle had been maintained that Jews cannot celebrate marriages otherwise than according to the rites of the Christian Church. The peculiar and fundamental tenets of their religion were adverse to their use of the rites of the Christian Church and distinguished their case materially from Dissenters, who acknowledged the same fundamental doctrines and did occasionally frequent the service of the

[1] See the note on p. 9 of the Appendix to Hag., *Cons.*, vol. I.

[2] 26 Geo. II, c. 34, s. 18.

Church. As to Quakers, the question had never been formally decided, but as to Jews it was unreasonable to maintain that their marriages according to their own rites should not be valid. If no Jewish marriage could be good, in all cases of intestacy the Crown would succeed to the effects which had never been obtained, although the Jews had long existed as a separate community. In overruling the objection, Sir William Wynne is reported to have said, "The objection taken is, as far as I know, perfectly novel. I do not recollect any case which I can name in which a Jewish marriage has been pleaded[1]; and I take it there has been no case in which a Jew has been called upon to prove his marriage. If there had, I conceive that the mode of proof must have been conformable to the Jewish rites, particularly since the Marriage Act, which lays down the law of this country as to marriages by banns or licence for all marriages had according to the rites of the Church of England and with an exception for Jews and Quakers. That is a strong recognition of the validity of such marriages. As to Dissenters there is no such exception, and no one would trust to the rules of their particular dissenting congregations for the validity of marriage. The comparison, therefore, between Jews and Dissenters does not hold, and more particularly in this that the Jews are Antichristian, the Dissenters Christian. Dissenters marry and Papists marry in the Church of England. In Haydon *v.* Gould the marriage was according to their own invention and the Prerogative Court refused to acknowledge that marriage. Here the parties are alleged to have been married 'according to the rites of the Jewish Church' and I am of opinion that this allegation is very proper to have been admitted[2]."

[1] The same judge in giving judgment in Lindo *v.* Belisario, in the Court of Arches, says that he was not aware of the case of Andreas *v.* Andreas, dealt with above, until it was mentioned during the argument.

[2] Vigevena & Silveira *v.* Alvarez (1794), 1 Hag., *Cons.*, Appendix, pp. 7 and 8, and note thereto.

A similar objection seems to have been taken in the proceedings for judicial separation brought against Baron D'Aguilar by his wife, which in the autumn of the same year came before the Consistory Court, presided over by Sir William Scott, afterwards Lord Stowell, but the objection was overruled upon the same grounds[1]. Shortly afterwards the same learned judge decided the well-known cases of Lindo *v.* Belisario and Goldsmid *v.* Bromer, and the validity of Jewish marriages became universally accepted[2]. The law on this point was held to be so certain and settled that, when the marriage law was revised in the year 1823, and Lord Hardwicke's Act repealed by the Marriage Act of that year, the marriages of Jews and Quakers are excepted from the provisions of the new Act in precisely the same terms as had been used in the earlier measure of 1753[3]. This, like the former Marriage Act, did not in terms, as did the later Act of 1836, declare the validity of these marriages, but was held to imply it by exempting them from its operation. It could, however, be argued that the true legal effect of such a clause, was to leave these marriages in precisely the same position as they had been at common law before the passage of the Acts. This view is distinctly maintained by Lord Campbell in his speech before the House of Lords in the case of the Queen *v.* Millis[4], in which, though the Law Lords were equally divided in opinion, the principle was finally laid down that the common law required the presence of a clerk in holy orders at every Christian marriage. The result of this decision and the speeches made by the Law Lords was to create a doubt as to the validity of the marriages of Jews and Quakers celebrated before the

[1] D'Aguilar *v.* D'Aguilar (1794), 1 Hag., *Ecc.*, p. 773; see also 1 Hag., *Cons.*, p. 134, note.

[2] Lindo *v.* Belisario (1795) is reported in 1 Hag., *Cons.*, 216, and Goldsmid *v.* Bromer (1798) in ibid., p. 324, and see Hopewell *v.* De Pinna (1808), 2 Camp., 113.

[3] See 4 Geo. IV, c. 76, s. 31.

[4] 10 Cl. & F. at p. 790.

The Marriage (Society of Friends and Jews) Act, 1847.

Marriage Act of 1836 came into operation. Accordingly, in the year 1847 Mr. Christie introduced and carried through Parliament "An Act to remove doubts as to Quakers' and Jews' marriages solemnized before certain periods" (10 and 11 Vict., c. 58). The Act, which is still in force, is in the following terms: "Whereas doubts have been entertained as to the validity of marriages amongst the people called Quakers and amongst persons professing the Jewish religion, solemnized in England before the first day of July one thousand eight hundred and thirty-seven, or in Ireland before the first day of April one thousand eight hundred and forty-five[1], according to the usages of those denominations respectively; and whereas it is expedient to put an end to such doubts; be it therefore declared and enacted &c. . . . That all marriages so solemnized as aforesaid were and are good in law to all intents and purposes whatsoever, provided that the parties to such marriages were both Quakers, or both persons professing the Jewish religion respectively."

Although this Act was rightly placed upon the statute book, from the arguments already stated and cases quoted there could have been but little room for doubt as to the validity of Jewish marriages, though Quakers' marriages were not in so strong a position. The true state of the case may be best seen from the statement of Lord Chief Justice Tindal in delivering the opinion of all the judges to the House of Lords in the case of the Queen *v.* Millis: "Since the passing of the Marriage Act it has generally been supposed that the exception contained therein as to the marriages of Quakers and Jews amounted to a tacit acknowledgment by the Legislature that a marriage, solemnized with the religious ceremonies which they were

[1] The days upon which the Marriage Act of 1836 (6 & 7 Will. IV, c. 85) and the Irish Marriage Act of 1844 (7 & 8 Vict., c. 81) respectively came into force. It should be noted that section 12 of the Irish Act is in precisely the same terms as section 2 of the English Act of 1836. This section, which relates to the marriages of Quakers and Jews, and expressly validates them, is specifically dealt with later.

respectively known to adopt, ought to be considered sufficient; but before the passing of that Act, when the question was left perfectly open, we find no case in which it has been held that a marriage between Quakers was a legal marriage by a contract *per verba de praesenti*; but, on the contrary, the inference is strong that they were never considered legal. . . . And as to the case of the Jews, it is well known that in early times they stood in a very peculiar and excepted condition. For many centuries they were treated not as natural-born subjects, but as foreigners, and scarcely recognized as participating in the civil rights of other subjects of the Crown. The ceremony of marriage by their own peculiar forms might therefore be regarded as constituting a legal marriage, without affecting any argument as to the nature of a contract of marriage *per verba de praesenti* between other subjects [1]."

No inference, however, as to the previous invalidity of Jewish marriages is to be drawn from the mere existence of this enactment. It is merely one of those numerous Marriage Confirmation Acts which are to be found scattered at frequent intervals in the statute book, and which have sometimes been enacted as much to remove the scruples of tender consciences as to solve genuine legal doubts. This particular Act was unquestionably introduced on account of some of the dicta let fall by the Law Lords in the case of the Queen *v.* Millis, but the only discussion which took place upon it in either House of Parliament consists of a statement by Sir George Grey, the Home Secretary of the day, that "he was assured by a very high authority that no such doubt as that alluded to . . . did really exist; but as some doubt had certainly been thrown

[1] 10 Cl. & F., pp. 671-3. The whole subject of the validity of Quakers' marriages before 1836 is dealt with in the Addenda to Roper's *Husband and Wife*, 2nd ed., vol. II, pp. 476 seq.; the effect of the clause in Lord Hardwicke's Act is excellently discussed at pp. 480-2. In the case of Haugton *v.* Haugton (1824), 1 Moll., 611, the Lord Chancellor of Ireland said that "as to the validity of a Quaker marriage, I have no manner of doubt."

out from the bench there could be no objection to the introduction of this Bill[1]."

The Act of 1847 confirms only Quaker and Jewish marriages contracted before the Marriage Act of 1836 came into force, because the express provisions of that Act with regard to these marriages were such as to remove all manner of doubt which could possibly be raised.

Provisions of the Marriage Act, 1836, as to Quakers and Jews.

It is now time to set these out in detail. Section 2 reads as follows: "The Society of Friends, commonly called Quakers, and also persons professing the Jewish religion, may continue to contract and solemnize marriages according to the usages of the said society and the said persons respectively; and every such marriage is hereby declared and confirmed good in law, provided that the parties to such marriage be both of the said society or both persons professing the Jewish religion respectively: provided also that notice to the registrar[2] shall have been given and the registrar's certificate shall have issued in manner hereinafter provided."

It is to be noted that this section expressly sanctions the continuance of marriages according to the usages of the Jews, and further declares all such marriages valid in case certain formalities are complied with, but it does not, nor does any other provision of English law, annul or declare invalid Jewish marriages where these conditions have not been fulfilled. The inference which is to be drawn is that if these marriages were valid before the passing of the Act they will still be legal after its enactment, for Jews may continue to contract them, but they are not declared good in law. In fact, the sentences of the section must be read disjunctively; the first part continuing and affirming the already existing privilege of Jews to celebrate their marriages in accordance with their own customs; the latter part conferring a new right upon Jews relating to the proof of their marriages. Hitherto if a Jewish marriage was in

[1] Hansard, *Parl. Deb.*, 3rd ser., vol. 91, p. 748.

[2] Now by virtue of 1 Vict., c. 22, s. 1, "the Superintendent Registrar."

dispute it had been necessary to produce evidence that the ceremonies required to constitute a marriage in accordance with Jewish usage had been performed; henceforth no such proof is necessary provided that the notice has been given and the certificate issued. In short, the conditions enumerated in the proviso must be complied with in order to entitle Jewish marriages to the benefit of the subsequent section 35, to which the words in the earlier section are naturally applicable. The material part of section 35, which has since been replaced and re-enacted by section 23 (see also section 17) of the Marriage and Registration Act, 1856, is as follows: "every marriage solemnized under this Act shall be good and cognizable in like manner as marriages before the passing of this Act according to the rights of the Church of England." Inasmuch as Jewish marriages had not hitherto been cognizable in the same way as Christian marriages, this interpretation gives ample meaning to the words in question.

Theory that the Marriage Act, 1836, renders invalid Jewish marriages in which the conditions laid down have not been complied with.

It is, on the other hand, frequently maintained that the effect of the proviso is much wider, and that it annuls and makes void all Jewish marriages in which the conditions are not fulfilled. Such marriages, it is said, are confirmed and declared good in law provided that the notice has been given and the certificate has been issued, and therefore if the notice has not been given or the certificate has not been issued they are declared null and void. The addition or interpolation of any such words, in a section of an Act of Parliament which can be completely interpreted without them, would be a violation of the principles of construction recognized in English law, and would moreover be peculiarly inappropriate and outrageous in the case before us. In the first place, the Marriage Act of 1836 was an enabling and not a disabling Act. Its object was to increase the facilities of marriage, and it created a new form of marriage, but did not abolish or restrict any of the old forms. Indeed, special care is taken to prevent the impression gaining ground that marriages heretofore legal had been invalidated by any of its provisions, for section 42, which declares certain marriages null and void, concludes with the following words: "Provided always that nothing herein contained shall extend to annul any marriage legally solemnized according to the provisions of an Act passed in the fourth year of his late Majesty George the Fourth, intituled An Act for amending the laws respecting the solemnization of marriages in England." Now Jewish marriages which took place before 1836 were undoubtedly held to be valid in consequence of the provisions of the Marriage Act of 1823 and Lord Hardwicke's Act of 1753, which it superseded, although in those times there was no registrar or superintendent registrar to receive the notice or issue the certificate. Not only are there no words in the Act expressly invalidating these marriages, but they are by the proviso in section 42 which has just been quoted saved from annulment by any words from which such a result might otherwise be implied.

Marriages previously valid are not made invalid by an Act of Parliament, unless it contains words expressly cancelling them.

Secondly, it is a well known principle of English law that the neglect or omission of any marriage ceremonies or formalities prescribed by a statute will not invalidate a marriage unless there are express words in the statute rendering it null and void. The best exposition of this principle will be found in the considered judgment of Dr. Lushington in the case of Catterall *v.* Sweetman[1]. That was a suit for nullity of a marriage which had taken place in New South Wales under a local Act of Parliament, which enabled Presbyterians to be married by their own minister instead of by a clergyman of the Church of England, "provided always that . . . no such marriage shall be had and solemnized until both or one of such persons as the case may be shall have signed a declaration in writing that he or she are or is a member of the Presbyterian Church, &c." The parties had been married by this form, but the declaration had not been signed. In delivering judgment,

[1] (1845), 1 Rob. Eccl., 304; see also p. 580, and 9 Jur., 954.

Dr. Lushington said: "The words in this proviso are negative words . . . they are certainly prohibitory of such marriages being had without the prescribed requisites, and no doubt the acting in disobedience of this law is a punishable offence; but whether the marriage itself is void, or only deprived of the validity given by the Act, is I feel a question of the greatest difficulty: there are no words annulling such marriage. . . . I have, amongst other inquiries, sought to discover if there is a case on record where any Court had pronounced a marriage null and void, unless there were words in the statute expressly so declaring it, and I can find none." He then goes through the different English Marriage Acts, and cases decided under them, and continues: "From this examination I draw two conclusions. First, That so far as my research extends it appears that there never has been a decision that any words in a statute as to marriage, though prohibitory and negative, have been held to infer a nullity, unless that nullity was declared in the Act. Second, That viewing the successive Marriage Acts it appears that prohibitory words without a declaration of nullity were not considered by the legislature as creating a nullity, and that this is a legislative interpretation of Acts relative to marriage." He then considers the provisions of the Colonial Act in question and the circumstances of the case, and holds that the marriage is not null and void, concluding as follows: "I think so firstly, because I find no instance of words in any Marriage Act being held to import a nullity, if the Act did not expressly create a nullity. Secondly, if this interpretation should be at variance with decisions of other Courts on other matters, it must always be remembered that marriage is essentially distinguished from every other species of contract whether of legislative or judicial determination; that this distinction has been universally admitted; that not only is all legal presumption in favour of the validity and against the nullity of marriage, but it is so on this principle, that a legislative enactment to annul a marriage *de facto* is a penal enactment, not only penal to the parties, but highly penal to innocent offspring, and therefore to be construed according to the acknowledged rule most strictly. Thirdly, I am confirmed in this opinion for this reason: the primary object of this New South Wales Act is remedial—to render indisputably valid past marriages; the second object is regulation—to determine what marriages in future shall be entitled to the benefit given by the Act. I consider, therefore, the regulation as restrictive of the benefit, that is, upon the legislative validity conferred by the Act, but leaving all other marriages as they stood before according to law[1]." The whole of this reasoning applies with still greater force to Jewish marriages celebrated in England after 1836, where the formalities imposed by the proviso of the second section of the Act of that year have not been complied with because the words of the section are merely declaratory, and not prohibitory as in the New South Wales Act.

Thirdly, if this contention were correct, a marriage according to the usage of the Jews, which was admittedly valid before the passing of the Act of 1836, would be in a worse position than marriages in Nonconformist chapels, which were undoubtedly null and void before that enactment. For a marriage of the latter kind is by section 42, as interpreted by the Courts, declared to be invalid only in case both the parties to it have knowingly and wilfully intermarried without fulfilling its essential conditions, and though there may have been material neglect in performing those conditions, including the regulations as to giving notice and obtaining the certificate, the marriage will still

[1] Dr. Lushington cites the cases of the King *v.* Birmingham (1828), 8 B. & C., 34, and Stallwood *v.* Tredger (1815), 2 Phill., 287, and reference should be made to the later case of Wing *v.* Taylor (1861), 2 Sw. & Tr., 278 at p. 286, also 30 L. J., P. & M., 263, where it was held that a marriage celebrated in the vestry of the church and in the presence of one witness only was valid, in spite of s. 26 of the Marriage Act of 1823.

be valid unless there is proof of a guilty knowledge of such neglect on behalf of *both* parties to it [1].

As a matter of fact, in the only case where this point in reference to a Jewish marriage has directly come before the Courts, Sir Francis Jeune, the late President of the Divorce Division, upheld the validity of the marriage, although no notice of the marriage had been given to the registrar. The case is too ill reported to be considered of high authority, and it may in fact have been decided on some other point; but on this one the judge is reported to have said: "Another objection to the validity of the marriage was that it had not been shown that notice had been given to the registrar as required by 6 & 7 Will. IV, c. 85, ss. 2, 3, and 4. It might be assumed that no such valid notice had been given, but even if that were so, even if the defendant had 'knowingly and wilfully' married contrary to the provisions of the statute, there was no evidence that such knowledge was shared by the deceased. Section 42 of 6 & 7 Will. IV, c. 85, clearly referred to section 2, and must be taken to apply to it. The cases of Greaves *v.* Greaves (L.R. 2 P. & D. 103), and the Queen *v.* Rea (L.R. 1 C.C.R. 365) went to show that 'both' parties to a marriage must be acting 'knowingly and wilfully' contrary to the provisions of the statute for the marriage to be void under the statute. The Irish case of '*In re* Knox' (23 L.R., Ir., 542) was not binding on the Court, but was entitled to respect as a high authority, showing as it did the interpretation which had been placed on the Act, 33 & 34 Vict., c. 110, ss. 38 and 39, which contained provisions very similar to those in 6 & 7 Will. IV,

Sir Francis Jeune's Dicta upon this question.

[1] See *In re* Knox (1889), 23 L.R., Ir. 542, and the Queen *v.* Rea (1872), L.R., 1 C.C.R. 365. These decisions are similar to those under the Act of 1823; as to marriages without due publication of banns or licence, see the very instructive case of Greaves *v.* Greaves (1872), L.R., 2 P. & D. 423, but it must be remembered that cases under the Act of 1823 do not necessarily apply to cases under the Act of 1836. See Holmes *v.* Simmons (1868), L.R., 1 P. & D. 523; and *In re* Rutter [1907], 2 Ch. 592, and the cases there cited.

c. 85. A marriage was not null and void unless the Act made it so. The words of 6 & 7 Will. IV, c. 85, did not make the defendant's marriage bad, and accordingly it was a good marriage[1]." The remarks of the learned judge are quoted at length because they may be thought to some extent to be in conflict with the construction of the statute as here laid down. However, the view here taken was not argued before the learned judge nor dealt with by him. In fact, he seems to have followed the argument of counsel for the defendant, who based their case, as it was unnecessary to go into the wider question, upon the provisions of section 42, and the point does not seem to have been taken by either counsel that that section applies only to persons intermarrying "under the provisions of this Act" (which words apply and may be confined to ss. 20 and 21, which admittedly have no relation to Jewish marriages), whereas upon the principles laid down in Catterall *v.* Sweetman Jewish marriages may still be solemnized under the law formerly in force without reference to the Act of 1836 at all[2]. However, it is not necessary to discuss this point minutely, as it is probably purely an academic one, for no case of an irregular Jewish marriage has as yet arisen or is likely to arise which would not be decided in precisely the same way whether the view of section 42 taken by Sir Francis Jeune or the principle of construction of section 2 here laid down be adopted.

The importance of complying with the requirements of the Marriage Act, 1836, in the case

It must not, however, be thought that the marriages of Jews without giving previous notice to the superintendent registrar and obtaining his certificate should be in any way countenanced or encouraged. Though they may not be illegal they are certainly irregular, and must always be subject to the grave defect that they are exceedingly difficult of proof in case they should ever come in question in any

[1] Nathan *v.* Woolf (1899), 15, *Times Law Reports*, p. 250.

[2] See especially the report of the case the second time it came before the Court on the question of divorce under the title of Catterall *v.* Catterall, 1 Rob. Ec. 580.

legal proceeding. They are, furthermore, in direct conflict with the spirit of the later English marriage laws, which contemplate the giving of notice in every case of marriage; indeed, section 4 of the Act of 1836 expressly enacts that "in every case of marriage intended to be solemnized in England after the first day of March according to the usages of the Quakers or Jews, or according to any form authorized by this Act, one of the parties shall give notice under his or her hand to the superintendent registrar of the district in which the parties shall have dwelt for not less than seven days then next preceding, or if the parties dwell in the districts of different superintendent registrars shall give the like notice to the superintendent registrar of each district," &c. Still this is what Austin calls a law of imperfect obligation, for the Act provides no sanction in case it is not complied with; but apart from the advantage in the matter of evidence to be obtained from compliance with the terms of the statute, people, and especially Jews, desire to obey statutory enactments even although no penalty is laid down for disregarding them[1].

of Jewish marriages.

It should be added that in one respect the Marriage Act of 1836 left the Jews as to their marriages in an inferior position to that of other Nonconformists, for section 11 of

A licence to solemnize a Jewish

[1] Section 39, from the earlier parts of which Jewish marriages are expressly excepted, makes certain cases of gross disobedience of the Act felony; the only crime thus created, which can be committed in the case of a Jewish marriage, is that "every person who shall knowingly and wilfully solemnize any marriage in England . . . (except by licence) within twenty-one days after the entry of the notice to the superintendent registrar . . . shall be guilty of felony." So that by the terms of the Act the celebrant of a Jewish marriage may be guilty of felony for disobeying the Act when notice has been given to the superintendent registrar, yet he is not guilty of any crime when the notice has been altogether omitted.

If section 42 is held to apply to Jewish marriages, the provision as to giving notice of Jewish marriages may be said to be not altogether without a sanction, for these marriages may be in some cases made invalid, but, as has been pointed out, these cases will be in practice of such rare occurrence that they can hardly be said to give a substantial sanction to the provision.

marriage could not be granted under the Act of 1836. This defect was remedied by the Marriage and Registration Act of 1856.

the Act empowered a superintendent registrar to grant licences for marriages to be solemnized either in a registered building within his district or his own office. This provision could not apply to a marriage in a Jewish synagogue, because a synagogue could not under section 18 be registered for solemnizing marriages, for in the year 1836 it could not be a building certified according to law as a place of religious worship[1], to which alone the section is applicable. The registrar is also precluded from granting a licence for a marriage to be solemnized in one of the churches of the establishment, but for such marriages an ecclesiastical licence can be obtained. Inasmuch as obtaining a licence makes it possible to shorten the period that must elapse before the marriage can be celebrated from twenty-one to seven days (and now by the Act of 1856 one whole day) from the time of giving notice, this was felt to be a hardship upon the Jews, and was accordingly remedied by section 21 of the Marriage and Registration Act of 1856, which expressly enables the marriages of Jews and Quakers to be solemnized by licence granted by the superintendent registrar to whom the marriage notice is given.

The registration of Jewish marriages.

The next point that arises for consideration is the registration of Jewish marriages; this is regulated by the Registration Act of 1836 (6 & 7 Will. IV, c. 86)[2], which immediately follows, and is to be read in conjunction with the Marriage Act of the same year. By the thirtieth section of that Act the registrar general is bound to furnish to every person whom the president, for the time being, of the London Committee of Deputies of the British Jews shall from time to time certify, in writing under his hand to the registrar general, to be the secretary of a synagogue in England of persons professing the Jewish religion a suffi-

[1] See *The Return of the Jews to England*, pp. 125, 126.

[2] This Act is given the short title of the Births and Deaths Registration Act, 1836, by the Short Titles Act of 1892 (55 & 56 Vict., c. 10), but it constantly refers to the registration of marriages as well as to the registration of births and deaths.

cient number in duplicate of marriage register books and forms for certified copies thereof, and such secretary must immediately after every marriage solemnized between any two persons professing the Jewish religion, of whom the husband shall belong to the synagogue whereof he is secretary, register or cause to be registered in duplicate particulars relating to the marriage according to the form set out in the schedule to the Act. He must further, whether he shall or shall not be present at the marriage, satisfy himself that the proceedings in relation thereto have been conformable to the usages of the persons professing the Jewish religion, and every such entry must be signed by the secretary, the parties married, and two witnesses. Every marriage secretary is further bound four times every year to deliver to the superintendent registrar, assigned by the registrar general, a true copy certified by him under his hand of all the entries during the quarter of marriages in the register kept by him, and, if there shall have been no marriage, to certify the fact under his hand[1], and to keep the marriage register books safely until they are filled. One copy of every such register book when filled is to be delivered to the superintendent registrar (to be subsequently transmitted to the registrar general), and the other copy is to remain under the care of persons professing the Jewish religion, to be kept with their other registers and records, and is for the purposes of the Act to be still deemed to be in the keeping of the secretary for the time being. The secretary is bound at all reasonable times to allow searches to be made of any register book in his keeping, and to give a copy certified under his hand of any entry or entries therein, and is entitled to fees, namely, for every search extending over a period not more than one year the sum of 1*s.*, and 6*d.* additional for every additional year, and the sum of 2*s.* 6*d.* for every single certificate.

[1] Sec. 28 of 7 Will. IV, and 1 Vict., c. 22, imposes a penalty of £10 for failure to comply with these requirements.

Offences in connexion with marriage registers.

Any secretary who refuses or without reasonable cause omits to register any marriage which he ought to register, or carelessly loses or injures any register book or certified copy thereof, or allows the same to be injured whilst in his keeping, is liable to forfeit a sum not exceeding £50 for every such offence. Moreover, sections 36 and 37 of the Forgery Act, 1861 (24 & 25 Vict., c. 98), which replace section 43 of the Registration Act, 1836, make it felony for any one, whether a marriage secretary or not, unlawfully to destroy, deface, or injure any marriage register or certified copy thereof, or to forge or fraudulently alter any entry therein, or to insert or permit to be inserted any false entry therein or in a copy required by law to be transmitted to the registrar or other officer, or to sign or verify any such copy which he knows to be false, or to take from its place of deposit or conceal any such copy for any fraudulent purpose.

Correction of erroneous entries in marriage registers.

Though fraudulent entries or alterations in the marriage register are thus severely punished, provision is made for the correction of accidental errors, for section 44 of the Registration Act of 1836 enacts that no person charged with the duty of registering any marriage, who shall discover any error to have been committed in the form or substance of any such entry, shall be liable to any of the penalties aforesaid if within one calendar month next after the discovery of such error in the presence of the parties married, or in case of their death or absence in the presence of the superintendent registrar and two other credible witnesses, who shall respectively attest the same, he shall correct the erroneous entry according to the truth of the case by entry in the margin without any alteration in the original entry, and shall sign the marginal entry, and add thereunto the day of the month and year when such correction shall be made; provided also that he shall make a similar marginal entry in the duplicate marriage register book and in the certified copy to be sent to the superintendent registrar, or if this shall already have been made then he must make and deliver a separate certified copy of the original erroneous entry and of the marginal correction.

The appointment of Jewish Marriage Secretaries.

The only persons capable of acting as Jewish marriage secretaries are under the Registration Act of 1836 such as are certified by the president for the time being of the London Committee of Deputies of the British Jews, generally known by its shorter title as the Board of Deputies, to be secretaries of synagogues. In order to ascertain whether any congregation of Jews desirous of having a secretary to register their marriages is a properly constituted synagogue, it is the invariable custom of the Jewish Board of Deputies to consult the chief rabbi or other ecclesiastical authority, and not to authorize their president to certify the secretary to the registrar general until a certificate stating that the congregation in question is a synagogue of persons professing the Jewish religion signed by the ecclesiastical authority is produced [1]. The Board of

[1] Thus, when a marriage secretary is to be appointed in place of one who has died or resigned, the president of the Board of Deputies can give the requisite certificate to the registrar general, enabling his successor in office to become a marriage secretary without consulting the members of the Board, but where a marriage secretary is to be appointed for a congregation which has not previously had such an officer, not only must the Board as a whole sanction the appointment, but a certificate from the ecclesiastical authorities must also be produced to prove that the synagogue is properly constituted. These conditions are imposed by bye-law 15 of the Board, which is in the following terms. "No secretary of any Synagogue, for which a secretary has not been previously certified to the registrar general by the president of the Board, shall be certified to the registrar general without the previous sanction of the Board, and due notice of the application shall be inserted in the summons convening the meeting at which the same will have to be considered." And clause 44 of the constitution of the same body, which provides that "In every future application to the Board to certify the secretary of a Synagogue under the Act 6 & 7 Will. IV, c. 86 or the Act 7 & 8 Vict., c. 81" (a similar act relating to marriages in Ireland), "for which no secretary has been previously certified by the president of the Board, such application shall be in writing, signed by the president and not less than five members of the congregation making application, and shall be accompanied by a certificate from the ecclesiastical

Deputies, which has thus received statutory recognition in respect of the appointment of marriage secretaries, was founded about the time of the accession of George III, and is the representative body of the Jews to which every recognized synagogue in the British empire is entitled to elect one or more delegates. Some few years after the enactment of the Marriage and Registration Acts of 1836 a considerable number of families of Jews seceded from the ancient Spanish and Portuguese congregation, and ultimately in the year 1842 established themselves as a separate body with a modified and reformed ritual under the title of the West London Congregation of British Jews. The Jewish ecclesiastical authorities refused to recognize the new congregation as a synagogue of persons professing the Jewish religion, and the president of the Board of Deputies accordingly declined to certify the secretary of the new congregation to the registrar general. In consequence any of its members who desired to have their marriage properly recorded and legally registered had perforce to first go through the civil form of marriage in a registry office and subsequently have the religious ceremony solemnized in the synagogue[1]. This inconvenience, which arose from the spirit of intolerance which at that time prevailed among the orthodox section of the Jewish community, was in due course remedied by the British Parliament, which was then espousing the cause of religious toleration. This was effected by section 22 of the Marriage and Registration Act of 1856, which conferred upon the members of the West London Synagogue and their

The West London Synagogue of British Jews.

authorities referred to in Clause 6 testifying that the applicants do constitute a Jewish synagogue."

[1] They could not require the presence of the registrar at the synagogue and be married there in his presence as provided by sec. 20 of the Marriage Act of 1836, because a Jewish Synagogue could not be registered under section 18 of the Act for the purpose of solemnizing marriages therein, for at this time it could not be a building certified according to law as a place of religious worship (see *The Return of the Jews to England*, pp. 125, 126).

secretary practically all the powers in relation to the registration of Jewish marriages which had been vested in the Board of Deputies by the Act of 1836. The section is as follows: "The registrar general shall furnish or cause to be furnished to the person whom twenty householders, professing the Jewish religion and being members of the West London Synagogue of British Jews, shall certify in writing under their hands to the registrar general to be the secretary of the West London Synagogue of British Jews, and also to every person whom such secretary shall in like manner certify to be the secretary of some other synagogue of not less than twenty householders professing the Jewish religion, and being in connexion with the West London Synagogue, and having been established for not less than one year, a sufficient number in duplicate of marriage register books and forms for certified copies thereof; and every secretary of a synagogue to whom such books and forms shall be furnished under this Act shall perform the same duties in relation to the registration of marriages between persons professing the Jewish religion as under an Act passed in the session of parliament held in the sixth and seventh years of his late Majesty King William the Fourth, chapter eighty-six, intituled, 'An Act for registering Births, Deaths, and Marriages in England,' are to be performed by the secretary of a synagogue to whom marriage register books and forms for certified copies thereof have been or shall be furnished under that Act."

This power of certifying marriage secretaries, conferred by the Act of Parliament on the secretary of the West London Synagogue, has been very jealously guarded by the council of that congregation, by whom it is in fact exercised[1]. Up to the present time it has been very

[1] By Law 89 of the West London Synagogue of British Jews the secretary "shall perform, in relation to the Registration of Marriages, the duties mentioned in the 22nd section of 19 & 20 Vict., c. 119; but he shall not certify, in pursuance of the section, without the authority

sparingly employed, and only two provincial synagogues, one at Manchester and one at Bradford, have secretaries certified under the provisions of this section.

The Secretary of a Synagogue cannot be "an authorized person" under the Marriage Act of 1898.

It has been suggested that it is possible for a congregation of Jews to escape the jurisdiction both of the Board of Deputies and of the Council of the West London Synagogue of British Jews in regard to marriages by constituting their secretary or other officer "an authorized person" within the meaning of the Marriage Act of 1898, and so enabling him to obtain from the registrar general the requisite marriage register books and forms under section seven of that statute. But this result cannot be attained under the terms of the Act because a "registered building," the trustees or other governing body of which can alone certify an authorized person, is strictly defined as a building registered for solemnizing marriages therein under the Marriage Act, 1836; and, as has been already stated[1], a Jewish synagogue could not be so registered under section 18 of that Act, for there was no legal provision in existence in the year 1836 for certifying a Jewish synagogue as a place of religious worship as required by that section. Several attempts to obtain the registration of synagogues under the Marriage Act of 1836, with a view, no doubt, to subsequently bring into operation the provisions of the Marriage Act of 1898, have been made, but the registrar general has finally decided that a Jewish synagogue cannot be legally registered for such purposes[2].

The proof of a Jewish marriage.

The registration of marriages, the machinery for which in the case of Jewish marriages has been described, is instituted for the purpose of facilitating their proof. This subject, the proof of a Jewish marriage, must now be more particularly discussed. As a general rule the pro-

of the Council, any person to be the secretary of a synagogue in connexion with the synagogue."

[1] See note 1 to p. 38.

[2] See *The Annual Report of the London Committee of Deputies of the British Jews*, April, 1898, pp. 14–15, and ibid., April, 1904, pp. 16–18.

duction of the register or a certified copy of it, together with sufficient evidence to identify the parties mentioned in the register, will be the most convenient method of proving a marriage[1]. But it is not necessary to adduce this form of proof in all cases. Dr. Lushington, in delivering judgment in Woods *v.* Woods, says: "I am of opinion that the register is not, in contemplation of law, the best evidence for three reasons; first, that registration is not necessary for the marriage itself (he had previously said in the same case, where the legality of a marriage is in question, it has been decided that, even if the marriage be not registered at all, if the fact of marriage can be proved, the non-registration will not affect its validity); secondly, that no error or blunder in the register could affect the validity of the marriage; and thirdly, that registration is not like an agreement or a deed in writing, the contents of which cannot be proved by viva voce evidence, but it is a mere record afterwards of what has been done, and, no doubt, a very important record to those who enter into the compact; but it is a mere memorandum of the compact they enter into, not the compact itself. I am encouraged in this opinion by the course of practice in the courts of law, which consider that, in order to establish a marriage, the evidence of any one person present at the marriage is sufficient, without calling for the register at all[2]."

Presumption of marriage.

Indeed, except in a few special cases, such as an indictment for bigamy or a suit for dissolution of marriage on the ground of adultery, or for restitution of conjugal rights, it will be sufficient proof of a valid marriage to show that two persons lived together and acknowledged each other as man and wife, for in such a case, unless the contrary be proved, the law will presume that a valid ceremony of marriage

[1] 6 & 7 Will. IV, c. 86, s. 38, "All certified copies of entries purporting to be sealed or stamped with the seal of the said Register Office shall be received as evidence of the birth, death, or marriage to which the same relates, without any further or other proof of such entry," &c.

[2] Woods *v.* Woods (1840), 2 Curt. 516 at pp. 520, 522.

has taken place, and this presumption of law will still be recognized in spite of the greater facilities of proof which the modern system of the registration of marriages has introduced [1]. This presumption in favour of marriage is so strong that it has been held to extend to the case of a Jew and a Christian cohabiting together and still adhering to their own religions. Thus in the case of Goodman *v.* Goodman evidence was produced to the effect that Isaac Goodman and Charlotte Geering resided together and cohabited, partly in England and partly in Belgium, from about the year 1804 to the death of the latter in the year 1832, that they were considered husband and wife, and that the children born of the union were registered as born in wedlock, but no evidence was given of the solemnization of any marriage between them. Although the relatives of Isaac Goodman swore that they never recognized the marriage, and some of them that they had never heard that it was reported to have taken place, it was held upon the weight of evidence and affirmed on appeal that it must be presumed that a marriage had taken place between Isaac Goodman and Charlotte Geering, and that the children of their union were legitimate and entitled to a share in a fund settled upon Isaac Goodman's next of kin [2].

[1] See Sastry Velinder Aronegary *v.* Sembecutty Vaigalie (1881), 6 A. C., 364, and *In re* Shephard [1904], 1 Ch. 456. The latter case seems to go too far, if it is to be assumed (as Kekewich (J.) did, see p. 462) that the marriage, presumed to have taken place in France, was impossible according to French law. It should be added that a marriage may be established by reputation, though one of the parties to it denies it. See Elliott *v.* Totnes Union (1893), 57 J. P. 151.

[2] Goodman *v.* Goodman (1859), 28 L. J., Ch. 745, and 4 Jur., N.S. 1220, and 5 ibid., 902. The will of Henry Goodman, the father of the said Isaac, was productive of a large amount of litigation. See in addition to the case already cited, Goodman *v.* Goodman (1847), 1 D. G., and Smale, 695; Goodman *v.* Goodman (1862), 3 Giff. 643, and there was further litigation on the death of his daughter Rachel as to who were entitled to succeed to her property as her next of kin. See *In re* Goodman's Trusts (1880), 14 Ch. D. 619, and on appeal 17 Ch. D. 266.

How a Jewish marriage is proved.

In cases where the fact of marriage will not be presumed and where proof of registration in accordance with the Registration Acts is not available, it will be necessary to prove first the formalities which were gone through, which must be done by a witness who was present at the ceremony, and, secondly, that those formalities constitute a valid marriage according to Jewish law. This latter is a question of fact which must be proved in every case in the same way as the principles or effect of any other foreign law are proved; i. e. by one or more expert witnesses learned in that law. As a general rule the best witness will be a Jewish rabbi, and it will be of advantage to have his opinion confirmed by the decision of a Beth Din or Jewish ecclesiastical court of three persons learned in Jewish law, but such evidence is not absolutely necessary; for the testimony of any person skilled in Jewish law may be accepted, and in the case of a difference of opinion or conflict of evidence among the witnesses the Court is entitled to form its own judgment as in any other case of disputed facts[1].

Formalities necessary for a valid marriage according to Jewish usage.

The requirements of the Jewish law, which may have to be formally proved in every case, are enumerated by the late Chief Rabbi, Dr. Nathan M. Adler, in his written statement furnished to the Royal Commission on the laws of marriage appointed in the year 1865, as follows: "Two fit and proper persons must be present during the solemnization of marriage and attest the same.

"The religious ceremony consists:—

"(*a*) Of the putting of the ring on the finger of the bride by the bridegroom, while pronouncing the words, 'Thou art wedded unto me according to the law of Moses and Israel.'

"(*b*) The pronouncing of the benediction by the minister

[1] See Lord Stowell's judgment in Lindo *v.* Belisario (1795), 1 Hag., *Cons. Cas.*, at p. 238, and pp. 259-60.

before and after the marriage vow (alluded to in Genesis xxiv. 60 and Ruth iv. 11, 12).

"(*c*) The publication of the marriage contract (alluded to in Tobit vii. 13, 14)."

But to constitute a valid marriage according to the usage of the Jews, the first mentioned ceremony (*a*) which is known as kedushim, if followed by consummation, is the only essential one, for though the others are omitted the marriage will still be binding, for marriage, although regarded as a divine institution and proper to be sanctioned by the blessing of religion, may be contracted in the absence of a rabbi or other minister of religion, provided that two competent witnesses are present[1]. "The essential portion of the marriage ceremony is, that the bridegroom places a ring on the finger of his bride, in the presence of two fit and competent witnesses, while pronouncing the words in Hebrew: 'Behold, thou art wedded (literally consecrated) unto me by this ring, according to the law of Moses and of Israel[2].'"

[1] The presence of two competent witnesses is essential to the validity of a marriage ceremony. No ceremony performed in their absence can be binding. "According to the Talmudic Law, only males who are of age, of sound mind and of moral character, are, in general, regarded as competent to act as witnesses. Besides, the witnesses may be closely related neither to each other, nor to either of the parties to the marriage." See Mielziner on the Jewish law of Marriage and Divorce, § 41.

[2] Per Dr. Hermann Adler in Hammick's *Law of Marriage*, p. 369. He adds: "This Act is preceded and followed by prayers and benedictions offered up by the minister who solemnizes the ceremony, in which the blessings of heaven are invoked upon the bridal couple.

The marriage covenant is read, in which the bridegroom declares to his bride 'I will honour and cherish thee; I will work for thee; I will protect and support thee, and will provide all that is necessary for thy due sustenance, even as beseemeth a Jewish husband to do.' It also sets forth that the bride has plighted her troth unto her affianced husband in affection and in sincerity." But though these further ceremonies are usual, they are not essential to the validity of the marriage. See also Mielziner on the Jewish law of Marriage and Divorce, § 51. The form of the Ketuba or Marriage Contract is given in the same work, § 49. See also *Jewish Encyclopedia*, VII, 472.

In two well-known cases of jactitation of marriage, the question of the formalities necessary to constitute a marriage according to the usages of the Jews has been directly raised. The first of these is Lindo *v.* Belisario, which was tried before Lord Stowell in 1795 and afterwards affirmed on appeal to the Court of Arches. In that case it was proved that on the 26th of July, 1793, between eleven and twelve o'clock in the morning, Esther Lindo, who was then unmarried and sixteen years of age, and Aaron Mendes Belisario, aged twenty-six or twenty-seven and a bachelor, went to the house of the latter's brother in Little Bennet Street, and there in the presence of Abraham Jacobs and Lyon Cohen, two credible persons of the Jewish nation, he (Belisario) said to Esther Lindo, "Do you know that by taking this ring (meaning a ring which he then produced to her) you become my wife?" to which she answered, "I do." He then said to her, "Do you take this ring freely, voluntarily, and without force?" to which she answered, "I do"; thereupon, in the presence of the witnesses, the said Aaron Mendes Belisario delivered to and placed the ring upon the forefinger of the left hand of the said Esther Lindo, which she tendered to him for that purpose, and she freely and voluntarily accepted and received it, and at the same time he repeated to her certain words in the Hebrew language, which were the well-known formula already set out. After hearing several witnesses skilled in Jewish law, and receiving the written answers to certain questions put by the Court to the members of the Beth Din, it was held that this ceremony did not constitute a binding marriage, because there had been neither consummation nor any nuptial benediction or any other of the ceremonies known as Chuppa. According to the evidence it was a betrothal, or at the most an inchoate marriage, which might prevent the parties from marrying again until a divorce was given, but it did not give the man any authority over the woman's fortune or person, rights which

The case of Lindo *v.* Belisario, 1795.

are the necessary consequences of marriage according to English law [1].

The case of Goldsmid v. Bromer, 1798.

The second case, that of Goldsmid *v.* Bromer, came before the same judge in the year 1798. The facts proved were that on the 22nd of November, 1795, David Bromer and Maria Goldsmid, then sixteen years of age, the daughter of the well-known financier, met by appointment and went in a coach to the Shakespeare Tavern in Covent Garden, where two persons were in readiness as witnesses. In their presence the Hebrew words which constitute the ceremony of Kedushim were pronounced, and this was followed by cohabitation between the parties. Accordingly, as consummation had taken place, the marriage could not be effectively impugned upon the ground, successfully taken in the former case, that Kedushim alone could not create a valid marriage. It was, therefore, objected that the witnesses were incompetent, and contended that the marriage was for that reason invalidated. After hearing evidence of the Jewish law the Court upheld this objection, and pronounced against the validity of the alleged marriage on the ground that it is essential to a binding Jewish marriage that it should be attested by two competent witnesses, and that of the witnesses to the ceremony in question one was disqualified by Jewish law on the ground of non-conformity, it having been proved that he had profaned the Sabbath, eaten forbidden meats, and stated that he was no Jew, but considered himself as bound only to the exterior observances of the religion in compliance with the wishes of his father, while the other (who was Bromer's first cousin) seems also to have been disqualified (though it was not necessary to decide the point) by reason of his relationship to one of the parties. This decision was afterwards affirmed on appeal both by the Court of Arches and the Court of Delegates [2].

[1] 1 Hag., *Cons. Cas.*, pp. 216-61, and ibid., Appendix, pp. 7-24.

[2] 1 Hag., *Cons. Cas.*, pp. 324-36.

It must be remembered that both these decisions were arrived at on the evidence placed before the Court, and are really judgments of fact and not of law. They are not binding precedents, and would not necessarily be followed if similar facts were proved; for instance, it is by no means certain that a witness to a Jewish marriage would be held incompetent because he was proved to have eaten food that was not kosher. They are, however, valuable as showing the principles on which the Courts will act.

Theory that a Ketuba or written contract is necessary to the validity of a Jewish marriage.

It is sometimes said that in order to prove a Jewish marriage where there has been no registration, it is necessary to produce the ketuba or written contract of marriage, and several charges of bigamy have been withdrawn from the jury at the Central Criminal Court because the first marriage having been celebrated abroad according to the usages of the Jews the prosecution have been unable to produce such a document[1]. But these cases cannot be considered authoritative, they were not decided by a judge of the High Court, and the ruling of law was given on the authority of a case which does not, when scrutinized, warrant it. The case is that of Horn *v.* Noel which was tried before Lord Ellenborough in 1807. It was an action upon a bill of exchange, in answer to which the defendant stated that she was a married woman, and therefore not liable under the old common law in force before the Married Woman's Property Acts, and two witnesses were called, who swore that they were present in the Jewish Synagogue, in Leadenhall Street in the year 1781, when the defendant was married by the high priest to Henry Noah, who had since taken the name of Noel and was still alive. Thereupon counsel for the plaintiff contended that this evidence was insufficient, and that it was necessary also to prove a written contract. The contract in the Hebrew language was accordingly put in and the plaintiff

[1] See Reg. *v.* Althausen (1893), 17 Cox 630. Reg. *v.* Nassilski (1897), 61 J. P. 520.

was non-suited[1]. There was in truth no ruling of law at all; an objection was taken by one of the counsel in the case, this was immediately satisfied by the other side, and that was the end of the matter. On the other hand, in giving judgment in the case of Nathan *v.* Woolf, the late Sir Francis Jeune expressly held that there might be a valid Jewish marriage even though there was no written contract at all[2], and in the leading case of Lindo *v.* Belisario Lord Stowell dealt with this point and on the evidence before him, and in particular on the strength of a certificate given by the Beth Din in respect of the marriage of one Benjamin Mendes Henriques in the year 1776 decided that, though there were no ketuba or sacred benedictions and blessings, a Jewish marriage might be good and valid[3]. The ketuba is, in fact, a marriage settlement rather than a marriage contract, and though it usually accompanies it is not an essential part of the Jewish ceremony of marriage[4].

The English Courts will not take judicial notice of the Jewish marriage law.

To sum up the English Courts will not take judicial notice of the Jewish marriage law, although it is recognized in the Marriage Acts, but will require it to be proved in every case in the same way as foreign law has to be proved, and if the marriage has taken place out of the jurisdiction, then it must, at least if it is in a country with a recognized system of law, also be proved that the marriage is valid by the law of that country[5].

[1] Horn *v.* Noel (1807), 1 Camp. 61.

[2] Nathan *v.* Woolf (1899), 15 Times L. R. 250. In the more detailed report in the *Jewish Chronicle* of March 17, 1899, Sir F. Jeune is reported to have said: "From the evidence last given it appears clear that the contract is one thing and the form of marriage another, and that the form of marriage constitutes a valid marriage, even though there is no contract at all. The contract is in point of fact more a civil matter in order to provide maintenance rather than that it goes to the essence and validity of the actual marriage."

[3] 1 Hag., *Cons. Cas.*, pp. 227–30.

[4] For the Ketuba see Mielziner, §§ 48–50. It is also discussed in the case of Montefiore *v.* Guedalla [1903], 2 Ch. 26.

[5] See the note on the case of Reg. *v.* Weinberg (1898), 33 L. J. (Notes), 239.

Consequences of the differences between English and Jewish law in the table of prohibited marriages.

There are certain marriages, such as one between uncle and niece, and formerly one between a man and his deceased wife's sister, which are permissible by Jewish law, but which are prohibited by the law of England. Such marriages will not be valid if they are contracted by Jews in accordance with Jewish rites and ceremonies, for the special privileges accorded to Jews extend only to the form of the marriage contract, and do not confer any status or capacity upon British subjects who profess the Jewish religion which is not shared by their Christian fellow subjects[1]. On the other hand, some marriages, which are permissible by English law, are forbidden by Jewish law; for instance, a man who has divorced his wife on the ground of adultery may not remarry her, if she has married another husband and is free to marry again on account of having become a widow or having been divorced a second time[2]. Again, the members of the priestly clan or descendants of Aaron, who often, though not always, bear the family name of Cohen, are forbidden to marry a divorced woman or any one who is not a member of the house of Israel[3]. Although since the destruction of the Temple the Jewish priesthood has ceased to exist, according to the usages of the Jews the Aaronites

[1] The marriage will not be validated by the parties to it going abroad for its celebration. See the recent case of *In re* De Wilton, De Wilton *v.* Montefiore [1900], 2 Ch. 481.

[2] See Deut. xxiv. 1–4, and compare Jeremiah iii. 1.

[3] In Leviticus a distinction is drawn between the ordinary priests or Aaronites and the high priest. In ch. xxi. 7: "They (the priests) shall not take a wife that is a whore or profane; neither shall they take a woman put away from her husband: for he is holy unto his God." Whereas in ver. 14 it is said of the high priest: "A widow or a divorced woman, or profane, or an harlot, these shall he not take: but he shall take a virgin of his own people to wife." But by the time of the Prophets an attempt seems to have been made to extend this stricter rule to all the priests, for it is said of them in Ezekiel xliv. 22: "Neither shall they (i.e. the priests, the Levites, the sons of Zadok, see ver. 15) take for their wives a widow, nor her that is put away: but they shall take maidens of the seed of the house of Israel, or a widow that had a priest before." But this attempt was not successful and the stricter rule has not been adopted by the authorized exponents of Jewish traditional law.

still retain their ancient privileges in the synagogue, and according to Jewish law and custom this particular disability still attaches to them. In consequence, a marriage between a Cohen and a proselyte or a divorced woman will not be celebrated in a Jewish synagogue or by a Jewish rabbi. Even the Reform synagogues, which do not recognize the special privileges of Cohanim, rightly decline to perform these marriages upon the ground that there is grave doubt as to their legality. Persons who desire to contract such marriages are directed by the authorities of such congregations to have a civil marriage before the registrar, and in some few cases a religious ceremony has afterwards been performed in the synagogue. In such cases the religious ceremony does not and is not intended to constitute a legal marriage, the parties to it being already man and wife in consequence of the proceedings before the registrar. Without the civil proceedings it would seem upon principle, for there is no direct authority on the point, that such a marriage would be null and void; for though the privilege given to the Jews by the Marriage Acts relates only to the forms and ceremonies of marriage, those who avail themselves of it must strictly comply with the terms on which it is granted. The terms are that the marriage must be contracted according to the usages of the Jews, and it is not in accordance with the usages of the Jews if one of the parties to it is prohibited by Jewish law and custom from marrying the other. It was held in Bromer *v.* Goldsmid[1] that a Jewish marriage was invalid because it was not witnessed by two persons duly qualified by Jewish law; *a fortiori* must such a marriage be invalid, if the parties to it are incapable of intermarrying by Jewish law. The law of England confers a special privilege upon Jews in recognizing the validity of their marriages celebrated in accordance with their own usages, although the formalities gone through would not, according to the ordinary law, constitute a binding marriage, but if Jews avail themselves of this privilege they must comply

[1] 1 Hag., *Cons. Cas.*, 324, vide supra.

with the requirements of Jewish law, which are in such case also requirements of the law of England.

Erroneous theory that marriages permitted by English law but prohibited by Jewish law cannot in any case be contracted by Jews domiciled in England.

It is held by some that these marriages, which are prohibited by Jewish law, cannot in any case be validly contracted by Jews even although celebrated under those provisions of the Marriage Acts which are not confined to Jews, as for instance, in a registry office without any religious ceremony. This view has been strengthened by the case of Meczyk *v.* Meczyk which was recently before the Divorce Court. In that case the marriage had taken place by certificate before the registrar in the Whitechapel Registry Office under the Marriage Act of 1836, and it had been proposed to have a religious ceremony in the synagogue, but before this took place the husband told the wife that he was a Cohen, and that as she was a divorced woman he could not marry her by Jewish law; he accordingly deserted her and afterwards committed adultery. The wife presented a petition for divorce, and the husband did not defend the suit. Upon these facts being proved, Mr. Justice Bargrave Deane is reported to have said that he was not satisfied that there was a valid marriage, and he therefore adjourned the case for further evidence. At the adjourned hearing no further evidence was called, and the judge again adjourned the case saying that, although he thought the wife was entitled to relief, yet the marriage was not proved to be a legal one, and if there was no marriage to dissolve the decree should be one, not of divorce, but of nullity of marriage. At the final hearing the judge made a decree nisi, dissolving the marriage, on the ground that there was no evidence that the husband belonged to the priestly family of Cohen, and was therefore disabled from contracting the marriage by Jewish law [1].

It will thus be seen that the judge did not deliver any judicial ruling in the case, and it is submitted that there is no justification for holding such a marriage invalid,

[1] See Meczyk *v.* Meczyk, reported in the *Times* newspaper, Oct. 25 and 31 and Nov. 7, 1905.

for in the first place the incapacity of the Aaronite to contract it will not necessarily be recognized by English law any more than the disability of persons who are bound by religious vows, or have entered religious orders, or are prohibited by the law of some foreign country under which they have been divorced from marrying again. In these and in similar cases the law of England will disregard the incapacity established by the law of a foreign country, because it is of a penal or religious nature which on grounds of public policy the law of England refuses to recognize or enforce[1].

In the second place the capacity of a person to make any contract (including marriage) in England is governed solely by the law of his domicile; if then a Jew is permanently resident in England, so as to have acquired a domicile there, his capacity to marry will be governed by the law of England only, and that law does not recognize any religious distinctions, and is the same both for Jews and Gentiles. Mr. Justice Stirling expressly held *in re* De Wilton that the exception made in favour of Jews by the Marriage Acts related only to the forms and ceremonies for celebrating a marriage, but did not extend to the capacity of the parties to contract[2]. In

[1] See Dicey on the *Conflict of Laws*, rule 122, pp. 474 seq., and Westlake's *Private International Law*, § 22 and § 16. It would appear that from the very earliest times a person who professed religion *in a foreign country* was not regarded here as "civiliter mortuus," see Co. Lit. 132 b. The right of a person divorced abroad, although prohibited by the decree of divorce from marrying again, to re-marry here was affirmed in the case of Scott *v.* the Attorney General (1886) 11 P. D. 128, which decision was explained in Warter *v.* Warter (1890) 15 P. D. 152.

[2] [1900] 2 Ch. 481, where it was held that the marriage of an uncle and niece, both domiciled British subjects, which was celebrated at Wiesbaden according to Jewish custom and practice, though valid by Jewish law was invalid as being prohibited by the law of England; similarly in Levy *v.* Solomon (1877), 25 W. R. 342, Vice-Chancellor Malins held that the subsequent marriage of Jewish parents in accordance with Jewish rites would not make their children already born legitimate, although Jewish law recognizes legitimation *per subsequens matrimonium*.

fine, if the marriages of Jews are celebrated in accordance with Jewish usages, by virtue of the special privileges conferred on the Jews by the Marriage Acts, the parties to them must not be prohibited from intermarrying either by English law or Jewish law, but if they are celebrated under the ordinary law by any of the forms which are open to Jew and Christian alike[1], they will be valid although they would not be sanctioned by Jewish law, provided that all the requirements of the English law have been satisfied.

Jewish irregular marriages.

It would not be right to conclude this essay without making some reference to a question which has long agitated the Jewish community of this country. In some cases Jews have contracted marriages according to their own rites without first giving any notice to the registrar or obtaining a certificate from him, and without having the marriage subsequently registered by a duly certified secretary of a synagogue. Such a union is known as Stille Chuppah or Stille Chosna. It has been already pointed out that such marriages, if the forms and ceremonies required by Jewish law have been duly complied with, are valid by the law of England, and in fact the marriages of all Jews in this country before the year 1837, when the Marriage and Registration Acts of 1836 first came into operation, were celebrated in this way. It is obvious, however, that such marriages are irregular and ought not to be encouraged, because they are in direct contradiction to the spirit of modern legislation regarding the registration of marriages, and furthermore great inconveniences may arise from the difficulty of proving such marriages, for where there is no registration, strict proof will be required, not only of what the requirements of the Jewish law are, but also that they have been duly complied with in the case in question. Indeed, in some instances, unscrupulous husbands have taken advantage of this difficulty, and deserted their wives with impunity.

[1] Jones, falsely called Robinson *v.* Robinson (1815), 2 Phill. 285.

Such conduct necessarily creates scandal, which reflects on the whole of the Jewish community, and yet no action has hitherto been taken by the Jews as a body to punish those of their number who thus set at nought their marital obligations. The excuses made for this inactivity are that some think that the law is not strong enough to deal with such cases, while others believe that the publicity, which would necessarily be given to them, would do great harm to the whole Jewish community. It would seem, however, that the only way to stamp out this evil, which if not checked may become so rampant as justly to arouse public indignation against those who, while cognizant of it, had done nothing to prevent it, is by bringing to justice and making an example of the wrongdoer in every case, so that it may be known as widely as possible that the duty of a husband to maintain his wife, which the law of the Jews insists upon with no less rigour than the law of the land, cannot be lightly neglected or defied. If, then, the view here expounded that these marriages are valid in law is correct, the writer is of opinion that wives deserted in this way should in all cases be assisted to obtain maintenance orders against their husbands, either under the Summary Jurisdiction (Married Women's) Act, 1895 (58 & 59 Vict., c. 59), or by proceedings in the Divorce Court, and if these orders are not complied with, or in a proper case, in the first instance the wife should be allowed to become chargeable to the parish in order that the provisions of the Vagrancy Act (4 Geo. IV, c. 83) may be rigidly enforced against the defaulting husband; who under that Act can be sentenced to various terms of imprisonment, and in the case of a third conviction to corporal punishment. The sole objection to this system is that it would introduce an exception to the principle of supporting its own deserving poor, which the Jewish community has so long and honourably maintained. If it is thought essential to remove this objection, which is no doubt a serious one, it may be pointed out that there would probably be little difficulty in obtaining a slight amendment of the Vagrancy Act in such a way as to extend its penalties so as to embrace persons who cause their families, by reason of their wilful neglect to maintain them, to become chargeable to a Jewish Board of Guardians[1].

Proposal to make the solemnization of such marriages a felony.

If the writer's view of the law is incorrect, then some other remedy should be sought, but the legal point should first be tested in the regular and proper way. There are some who think that without testing the legal point legislation should at once be asked for declaring these marriages invalid and enacting the penalties of felony against all those who take part in celebrating them. Without discussing the propriety of attempting to obtain such a change in the law or its likelihood of success, if it were carried out it might cause great hardship and injustice. The parties to these marriages are almost always foreigners, and the ceremonies performed unquestionably constitute valid marriages according to the law of many if not most foreign countries. It would be unfair to visit with such severe punishment poor and ignorant persons (for it is amongst this class only that these marriages take place) who, in spite of the fiction of our law that every one is presumed to know it and all the changes continually being made in it, might not be cognizant that they had committed any offence. Moreover, marrying without giving notice to a registrar is not in itself a moral offence, and should not be made a serious crime unless, from the surrounding circumstances, it can be inferred that the intention was to go through a mock ceremony of marriage or evade the obligations which marriage entails. That wife-desertion is made easy is the real evil of the Stille Chuppah—an evil which would not be diminished but rather increased by a legal declaration that such a ceremony

[1] In the extreme case of a man who has married in this way absconding from his wife and taking a second one, a prosecution for bigamy might be commenced, but it would then be necessary to prove strictly to the satisfaction of a jury the legal validity of the first marriage.

cannot constitute a binding marriage. The same objection may be advanced against merely subjecting to the penalties of the criminal law all persons who take part in or in any way aid and abet a ceremony of Stille Chuppah without formally declaring it to be invalid; for it is obvious that the result of such an enactment would necessarily be to deter all persons from coming forward as witnesses and so destroy the means by which the matrimonial obligation can be enforced. Let it be once known that a Stille Chuppah will not enable the duties entailed by marriage to be set at nought, and the most serious evils resulting from these irregular marriages will disappear. It is no doubt to be wished, for reasons already stated, that these marriages should be wholly discontinued; but unless the conditions of Jewish immigration from abroad are changed, this hope is not likely to be realized in the immediate future. In the meantime these marriages are in precisely the same legal position as irregular marriages in Scotland which are still recognized as valid in this country[1].

Qualified exemption of Jewish marriages from the provisions of the Marriage with Foreigners Act, 1906.

The Marriage with Foreigners Act, 1906, confers a new privilege upon Jews by exempting their marriages from the provisions of its second section. That section provides that, where the necessary arrangements have been made with any foreign country, an Order in Council may be made (*a*) requiring any person subject to the law of that foreign country, who is to be married to a British subject in the United Kingdom, to give notice of the fact that he is subject to the marriage law of that country to the person by whom the marriage is to be solemnized, and (*b*) forbidding any person to whom such a notice is given to solemnize the marriage or allow it to be solemnized until a certificate that there is no impediment to the marriage according to

[1] See Dalrymple *v.* Dalrymple (1811), 2 Hag., *Cons. Cas.*, 54. By Lord Brougham's Act, 1856 (19 & 20 Vict., c. 96) an irregular marriage contracted in Scotland will not be recognized as valid unless one of the parties has resided in Scotland for twenty-one days next preceding the marriage.

the law of the foreign country in question, is produced to him, and that any person acting in contravention of such regulations shall be guilty of a misdemeanour and liable to punishment by fine not exceeding £100 or imprisonment not exceeding one year. The object of this provision is to prevent the scandal, which has occasionally occurred, of a marriage between a British subject and a foreigner celebrated in this country being subsequently discovered to be void because the foreign spouse is by the law of his or her own country for some reason (unknown perhaps to the other party) incapable of contracting the marriage [1].

Jews coming from Russia, Roumania, Morocco or other places where the law does not accord the Jew equal rights with the rest of the population, if desirous of marrying here would labour under grievous disability by reason of the difficulty they would experience in obtaining the requisite certificate. Accordingly, on the representation of the Jewish Board of Deputies, the Government inserted a clause in the Act granting Jewish marriages a qualified exemption from its provisions; it is in the following terms:—

"Nothing in this section shall be taken to relate or have any reference to any marriages between two persons professing the Jewish religion solemnized according to the usages of the Jews in the presence of the Secretary of a Synagogue authorized by either the Births and Deaths Registration Act, 1836, or the Marriages (Ireland) Act, 1844, or by the Marriage and Registration Act, 1856, to register such a marriage, or of a deputy appointed by such secretary by writing under his hand and approved by the President for the time being of the London Committee of Deputies of the British Jews by writing under his hand [2]."

[1] For the hardships which may arise in such circumstances, see the recent case of Ogden *v.* Ogden [1907], P. 107.

[2] 6 Edw. VII, c. 40, § 2 (3). It will be observed that if the marriage is

The exemption does not apply to the marriages of Jews in a registry office or to the irregular marriages by Stille Chuppah, but only to marriages accompanied by a religious ceremony under the auspices of a recognized and duly certified synagogue. In the case of all such marriages it has long been customary both for the Chief Rabbis and the authorities of the West London Synagogue to make the necessary inquiries as to whether there is any impediment to the legality of the marriage when performed, more particularly when one of the parties is a foreigner, and strictly to refuse authorization in every doubtful case. The provisions of the Act are therefore unnecessary in the case of these marriages, but a new duty is thrown upon the Jewish community to see that the proper inquiries are efficiently made.

Jewish law of Divorce.

This essay may be brought to a conclusion without discussing the Jewish law of divorce which is founded upon the first verse of the twenty-fourth chapter of Deuteronomy, "When a man hath taken a wife and married her and it come to pass that she find no favour in his eyes because he hath found some uncleanness in her, then let him write her a bill of divorcement and give it in her hand and send her out of his house"; because by the common law of England a marriage once validly contracted can be dissolved only by the death of one of the parties to it. This principle of the common law can be overridden only by Act of Parliament, and though there are statutory enactments recognizing the validity of Jewish marriages there is none recognizing the validity of Jewish divorces; Jews domiciled in England can therefore only be divorced

solemnized in the presence of a deputy appointed by the secretary of a synagogue, his appointment must be approved by the President of the Board of Deputies, and that no provision is made for approval by an officer of the West London Synagogue in the case of a deputy of a marriage secretary under its jurisdiction. The reason for this is that it is the practice of the West London Synagogue to insist that its marriage secretaries should be present at all marriages and not to allow them to appoint a deputy.

by a Decree of the Court under the provisions of the Divorce Act, 1857. It should however be added that where a Jew or Jewess, who had been married according to Jewish usages, and divorced by a decree of the Divorce Court, desires to contract a second marriage in accordance with Jewish religious rites, it is essential that the original Jewish marriage should be first dissolved by a Jewish divorce, for otherwise the second marriage will be invalid on the ground that one of the parties to it is, according to Jewish law, incapable of contracting it[1].

[1] The whole system of Jewish divorce is fully explained in Amram's *Jewish Law of Divorce*. The invalidity of a Jewish divorce in England may be gathered from the report of the case of Moss *v.* Seth-Smith (1840), 1 M. & G. 228. On the other hand it may be said that a Jewish divorce was recognized as valid in the case of Ganer *v.* Lady Lanesborough (1791), 1 Peake, p. 17, but the divorce there in question took place at Leghorn, and it must be assumed that the parties to it were at the time domiciled at Leghorn, and that the law prevalent there recognized and adopted the principle that a Jewish marriage might be dissolved by a Jewish divorce. In the recent case of Friedberg *v.* Friedberg, Sir J. Gorell Barnes acted upon the principle that a rabbinical divorce pronounced in England has no effect upon a Jewish marriage; although the marriage may have been solemnized abroad. He accordingly dissolved a Jewish marriage celebrated at Riga in Russia on the ground of the bigamy and adultery of the husband, who had brought his wife to and acquired a domicile in England and there obtained a rabbinical divorce and afterwards gone through the form of marriage with another woman in Scotland. (See the *Jewish Chronicle* for Oct. 16, 1908.)